Unshackle Your Wings

Copyright © 2025 by Tessy Tanyi

Published by Four Rivers Media

All rights reserved. No portion of this book may be reproduced, stored in a retrieval system, or transmitted in any form or by any means—electronic, mechanical, photocopy, recording, scanning, or other—except for brief quotations in critical reviews or articles, without prior written permission of the author.

Unless otherwise specified all Scripture quotations are taken from the Holy Bible, New International Version®, NIV®. Copyright © 1973, 1978, 1984, 2011 by Biblica, Inc.™ Used by permission of Zondervan. All rights reserved worldwide. www.zondervan.com. The "NIV" and "New International Version" are trademarks registered in the United States Patent and Trademark Office by Biblica, Inc.™ | Scripture quotations marked AMP are taken from the Amplified® Bible (AMP), Copyright © 2015 by The Lockman Foundation. Used by permission. www.lockman.org | Scripture quotations marked ESV are from The ESV® Bible (The Holy Bible, English Standard Version®), copyright © 2001 by Crossway, a publishing ministry of Good News Publishers. Used by permission. All rights reserved. | Scripture quotations marked KJV are taken from the King James Version of the Bible. Public domain. | Scripture quotations marked MSG are taken from THE MESSAGE, copyright © 1993, 1994, 1995, 1996, 2000, 2001, 2002 by Eugene H. Peterson. Used by permission of NavPress. All rights reserved. Represented by Tyndale House Publishers, Inc. | Scripture quotations marked NKJV are taken from the New King James Version®. Copyright © 1982 by Thomas Nelson. Used by permission. All rights reserved. | Scripture quotations marked NLT are taken from the Holy Bible, New Living Translation, copyright © 1996, 2004, 2015 by Tyndale House Foundation. Used by permission of Tyndale House Publishers, Inc., Carol Stream, Illinois 60188. All rights reserved. |

For foreign and subsidiary rights, contact the author.

Cover design by: Tessy Tanyi
Cover photo by: Jenish

ISBN: 978-1-964794-76-1   1 2 3 4 5 6 7 8 9 10

Printed in the United States of America

Unshackle Your Wings

**DISCOVER YOUR TRUE IDENTITY
AND FULFILL YOUR DIVINE PURPOSE**

TESSY TANYI

Dedication

To every person who has ever doubted their worth or questioned their purpose: this book is for you. May you come to know the depth of God's love, the truth of your divine identity, and the freedom to soar as the kingdom eagle He created you to be.

To my family and friends who have supported me on this journey: your prayers, encouragement, and love have been my foundation.

And above all, to my Bridegroom, Savior, and King: thank You for calling me, equipping me, and giving me the courage to soar. This is for Your glory.

CONTENTS

Preface xi
Acknowledgments xiii
Introduction 15
CHAPTER 1. **The Eagle's Reflection** 23
CHAPTER 2. **The Awakening** 31
CHAPTER 3. **Identity Crisis** 47
CHAPTER 4. **Unmasking Identity Thieves** 57
CHAPTER 5. **The Eagle Within You** 71
CHAPTER 6. **Reflect and Rise** 85
CHAPTER 7. **Wings of Change** 101
CHAPTER 8. **Preparing for the Flight Ahead** 131
CHAPTER 9. **Soaring with Purpose** 147
CHAPTER 10. **Weathering the Storm** 163
CHAPTER 11. **Associations** 177
CHAPTER 12. **The Eagle's Gaze** 191
CHAPTER 13. **Rise Above the Battle** 205
CHAPTER 14. **Feeding the Eagle Within** 219
CHAPTER 15. **The Wilderness Experience** 235
CHAPTER 16. **From Hidden to Heralded** 253

CHAPTER 17. **The Majestic Eagle** **271**
CHAPTER 18. **Final Charge**.......................... **279**
About the Author....................................... *291*

PREFACE

An eaglet once fell from his nest, and a farmer found him, took him home, and placed him together with the chickens. The eaglet lived and grew along with all the other chickens, and whatever they did, the eaglet did too. He thought he was a chicken, so he began to think and act like one. The eaglet began clucking and pecking at some grains on the ground as the chickens did.

One day, the farmer's friend visited the farm, and when he saw the eaglet amongst the chickens, he said to the eaglet, "You are an eagle; you are meant for the heavens. What are you doing here with the chickens?" Hence, he picked the eaglet up and threw him in the air. The eaglet flapped his wings but fell to the ground and returned to the chickens. During his next visit to the farm, he saw the same eaglet with the chickens again. This time, he took the eaglet to the top of the barn and threw him in the air. The eaglet again flapped his wings, fell to the ground and, again, returned to the chickens. The farmer's friend was sad. When he visited the farm for the third time and saw the eaglet still with the chickens, he felt really sad, and so this time, he took the eaglet to the top of a mountain and threw him high in the air. The eaglet, very frightened, flapped his wings and fell downwards. As he was falling, he flapped his wings harder and harder until, suddenly, he soared up into the sky and disappeared. He had learned to fly.

The end of this story might sound exciting, but I do not want you to forget the purpose of the story:

If the farmer had not helped the eagle realize who he was, the eagle would have lived and died as a chicken.

Today, there are many individuals whose lives are like the eagle, suffering from what I call an identity crisis and living like a chicken. Trapped within many is a sublime bird of potential that may never fly.

Just like the farmer's friend, the principles in this book are designed to help you discover and reclaim your "unidentified" identity and discover the untapped potential locked up inside of you. This book will dare you to leave the beaten path of mediocrity and blaze adventurous new trails for the glory of God and the good of society. It will challenge you to live the truly majestic life of the eagle and leave footprints deep enough for others to follow in your generation and generations to come.

ACKNOWLEDGMENTS

First and foremost, I give all honor and glory to God. Without Your love, guidance, and unending faithfulness, this book would not exist. You have been my strength in every season, my wisdom in every decision, and my comfort in every challenge. Thank You for calling me, equipping me, and entrusting me with words to set others free.

To my beloved husband (Johnny Tanyi) and precious children (Lauren and Jayden): You are my living love letters from God. Johnny, your hands hold mine when writing grows heavy. My precious Lauren and Jayden, your childlike worship reminds me daily why these words matter—for your generation and the kingdom you'll inherit. Every page bears the fragrance of your patience through late nights and your joy that refilled my weary soul. You are my first ministry and crown.

To my precious mother, though our faith journeys bloomed in different seasons, your prayers have been golden bowls of incense before God (Revelation 5:8). Thank you for standing in the gap until my eyes opened—and for cheering me onward.

To my spiritual leaders: Pastor Atoe, Pastor Laurence, Pastor Greg: You became my Aaron and Hur (Exodus 17:12), holding up my arms when weariness came. Your teachings on following God wholeheartedly became manna during my wilderness walk. Thank you for pouring into my life, guiding me, and reminding me of my calling. Your wisdom and insights have been invaluable.

Friends who became siblings: You carried me through valleys with laughter and intercession. Special thanks to Nana Rennie, Temi Odeyale, and Grace Like Rain for all-night prayer calls and fellowship.

To the creative hands behind these pages: editors, designers, etc.—you're the Bezalels (Exodus 31:1-5) who shaped God's vision into tangible glory.

And finally, to you, dear reader, may the Lion of Judah roar through these pages, shattering lies and awakening your royal destiny. Run, sister. Soar, brother. The kingdom awaits your unshackled wings.

With eternal gratitude,
Tessy Tanyi

INTRODUCTION

Like Brennan Manning, I've learned I'm neither the brokenness others define me by, nor the piety they project—only a fellow traveler whispering, "The bread of grace is this way."[1]

𝓑rennan Manning knew the weight of a double life—he was a celebrated minister who fought a private battle with addiction. Sandra, an Ivy League lawyer, knew it too, confessing, "I won cases by day and cried in parking garages at night." Their stories expose a universal truth: we are all performers, wearing identities that no longer fit—if they ever did. The gap between who we pretend to be and who we truly are grows wider with every act, leaving us exhausted, empty, and aching for something real.

Startling research reveals 1 in 3 adults feel lost when asked, "Who are you beyond your job, title, or duties?"—their authentic selves buried under societal roles.[2] Additionally, according to Dr. Dena Bravata, up to 82 percent of people experience imposter thoughts at some point in their lives.[3]

---

1 Brennan Manning, *The Ragamuffin Gospel: Good News for the Bedraggled, Beat-Up, and Burnt Out* (Colorado Springs, CO: Multnomah, 2005).
2 American Psychological Association, "Stress in America: Identity Erosion in Modern Adulthood," 2022, https://www.apa.org/news/press/releases/stress; Gallup, "Global self-perception study: How work shapes identity," 2022, https://www.gallup.com/workplace.
3 Dena M. Bravata, et al., "Prevalence, Predictors, and Treatment of Imposter Syndrome: A Systematic Review," *Journal of General Internal Medicine* 35, no. 4 (2020): 1252-1275. https://doi.org/10.1007/s11606-019-05364-1.

Close your eyes. Who are you when no one needs you? For 33 percent of adults, this question triggers silence—not because they're empty but because they've been taught to define themselves through service, not being.[4] If this resonates, you're not broken—you're ready. In the coming pages, we will unearth the "you" that existed before the world gave you labels. This book is for the weary. For those ready to shed the costumes, silence the applause, and finally meet themselves. *Unshackle Your Wings* is not about becoming someone new. It's about uncovering who you were before the world told you who to be. Like Sandra, we've all stared into the mirror and seen a stranger. But this is more than a psychological struggle—it's spiritual identity theft, a replay of Eden's oldest lie: "You could be more . . ." (Genesis 3:5). The tragedy isn't that we're lost. It's that we've forgotten we were ever found.

MY JOURNEY: FROM RELIGION TO REVELATION

For years, I hungered for more than Sunday rituals. I turned my plate upside down—fasting, praying, crying out: "God, reveal Yourself to me!" And He answered. Slowly, like Paul, I began to grasp the "surpassing worth of knowing Christ" (Philippians 3:8).

But the church today? We've traded glory for formality. Billy Graham's warning rings truer than ever: "Our greatest need today is not more Christianity but more true Christians."[5]

---

4 APA, "Stress in America."
5 Billy Graham, "Our greatest need today is not more Christianity but more true Christians," *Craig T. Owens*, 28 Aug. 2012, https://craigtowens.com/2012/08/28/14-quotes-from-billy-graham-in-quotes/.

Where are the soldiers of righteousness? Where is the power to heal, deliver, and transform? Too many of us are eagles living like chickens—content with scraps when we're called to rule the skies.

THE QUESTION OF "WHO AM I?"

The question "Who am I?" haunts human hearts across every boundary of belief. The secular executive climbing the corporate ladder, the devout monk in silent prayer, the exhausted single parent, the teenager scrolling social media—all share this primal hunger for identity. We package ourselves with job titles, relationships, and achievements yet still feel like imposters in our own skin. Like I said, this isn't merely a psychological struggle; it's the spiritual echo of Eden, our souls remembering we were made for more than performance and perception. The Christian fights to reconcile her worth in Christ with her failures. The atheist wrestles with meaning in a purposeless universe. But both are answering the same fundamental cry—the cry God responds to when He whispers, "You are mine" (Isaiah 43:1).

A quiet epidemic of spiritual displacement runs through our pews and workplaces alike. Many devoted Christians confess they can recite verses about grace yet struggle to believe those verses for themselves. Others find their God-given worth tangled in career changes and cultural expectations as if identity were a job title to be rewritten every few years. These aren't just statistics—they're lived experiences echoing through confessionals, coffee shops, and late-night prayers. The common thread? We've become fluent in the language of divine love, yet illiterate in applying it to our own stories.

Even Maya Angelou documented her struggle of searching for who she was, even after writing seven autobiographies!

So, I ask you now, dear reader, with the same gentleness God used to awaken me to my true nature: *Who* do you see when you look in the mirror?

Much of the postmodern church is laden with a spirit of religion, complacency, and lukewarmness. We seem to have a form or appearance of godliness in a churchy culture, but what is missing are Christians who are manifesting the reality of heaven's power on earth. Underneath the layers of the verbosity of our religiosity, lie many burdens of sin and the overwhelming troubles of life. Illnesses and all forms of diseases are common among Christians; demonic spirits are ravaging families and even churches, and the armies of the Lord keep them unchecked. Where are the soldiers of righteousness, where are the wailing women, and where are the men of valor? Sometimes, I wonder if this is the abundant life that Jesus Christ promised. Is this the supernatural life of glory that we are meant to manifest as heaven's ambassadors in the earthly realm? It appears to me that the majority have lost their identities.

THE EAGLE'S CALL: WHY THIS BOOK MATTERS

God didn't liken us to eagles for pretty sermons. He chose this symbol because:

- » **Eagles soar above storms** (Isaiah 40:31)
- » **Eagles renew their strength** (Psalm 103:5)
- » **Eagles fear no heights** (Deuteronomy 32:11)

This book is *not* self-help fluff. It's a prophetic wake-up call for the remnant—those sick of shallow faith and hungry for authentic kingdom living.

More than ever, the church of Jesus needs to raise a voice of lamentation and say to the Lord, like Habakkuk the prophet of old, "O LORD, I have heard Your speech *and* was afraid: O LORD, revive Your work in the midst of the years! In the midst of the years make *it* known; In wrath remember mercy" (Habakkuk 3:2, NKJV). Unless we take this approach and wake up to our true identity in Christ, everything else is ritualistic, ceremonial.

God likens believers to eagles for a reason—not just to warm a church pew or to sound and look "spiritual" but to truly know who we are and to carry out His kingdom mandate. Throughout Scripture, the eagle symbolizes strength, renewal, and the ability to rise above challenges. Isaiah 40:31 reminds us that those who wait on the Lord will soar like eagles, while Exodus 19:4 and Deuteronomy 32:11 illustrate God's protection and guidance using the imagery of an eagle caring for its young. This book is neither just another "feel good, name it, claim it" self-help guide, nor is it merely a theoretical discourse or theological exposition. It is a call to revival—a call to seek God with a renewed passion until His glory is manifested in our lives. Just as an eagle was never meant to live like a chicken on the ground, we, as God's people, are called to rise, embrace our true identity, and walk in the fullness of His purpose.

A WARNING AND WELCOME

This book is specially written under the inspiration of the Holy Spirit for the remnant generation—those who are sick and tired of being sick and tired and want to leave the shallow waters and plunge into the depth of the river of life.

Put this book down if:
» You're satisfied with only ordinary things of life such as food, designer labels, and luxury cars but indifferent to God's glory.
» You prefer comfort over the cost of discipleship.

Keep reading if:
» You're ready to shake off mediocrity.
» You'll let this book unsettle you, transform you, and sever ties with anything that clips your wings.

The cliff's edge is here. The winds of the Spirit are stirring. Will you step off and soar—or retreat to the barnyard?

No matter how long you've traveled the wrong road, you can still turn back.

The sky awaits, eagle.

If you're still reading this book, it means you desire that Christ be formed in you and that His will be done through your limited days on earth. You have heeded the higher calling, and to you, shall all "these things" be added (Matthew 6:33) and much more. I welcome you to read along, and let us unravel heaven's mysteries together as they relate to the phenomenal eagle and our identity as believers. The book contains the tools you need to live the victorious kingdom life that God has destined for you to live. I call it "Kingdom Tools in a Box."

Caution! You hold a divine disruptor in your hands—this isn't another devotional to make you feel holy but a spiritual defibrillator charged to restart your dormant destiny. What happens when you keep reading? Your mediocrity will feel like a straitjacket—you'll either break free or throw this book across the room. God will whisper truths about you that make your knees buckle, just like an eagle recognizing its wings for the first time. That'll be you by chapter 3. Some relationships will start feeling like anchors because not everyone is meant to soar at your altitude.

Your Bible will burn in your hands as familiar verses detonate with new power.

Why eagles? Because you're not a chicken. God could have compared you to a loyal dog or busy bee, but He chose the eagle—the only creature that uses storms to reach higher. By the time you finish, you'll stop praying for easier storms and start riding God's currents. You'll trade "Who am I?" for "Whose am I?" You'll upset some people—which is good because revival always makes complacent Christians nervous.

This book is your invitation to lay down the masks—not to become someone new but to recognize who you've always been. Through these pages, we'll expose the lies that keep you small, rediscover the love that calls you worthy, and awaken the purpose your soul already knows. Freedom starts here.

The fact that you're still reading tells me everything. You're not looking for comfortable words to sip like a latte—you're ready for truth that will shatter your spiritual limitations. Can you feel it? The winds of awakening are stirring. This is your moment of divine decision, eagle. Will your fear and familiarity keep you earthbound, or will you spread your wings and claim your rightful place in the skies?

If you're ready to stop crawling and finally soar, turn the page—your transformation begins now.

CHAPTER 1

THE EAGLE'S REFLECTION

*Seeing Yourself
Through God's Eyes*

I ask you again, fellow eagle, with the same gentleness God used to awaken me to my true nature: who do you see when you look in the mirror?

Take a moment to truly reflect on that question. If you're anything like me—or like Sandra, a corporate lawyer who once confessed she felt like "an imposter in a suit" despite her Ivy League degree—you may see someone burdened by expectations, self-doubt, or the weight of not measuring up. But here's the life-changing truth: God's view of you is clearer, greater, and more loving than anything you or anyone else could imagine. There have been times when the reflection staring back at you didn't look like someone who was thriving or confident. Instead, you may have seen someone who felt like they weren't measuring up—someone staggering under the weight of expectations, whether those came from others or your own harsh self-criticism. I've been there, and it's not an easy place to be. But here's one thing I've learned: the person we see in the mirror depends on the mirror we are looking at.

THE MIRRORS WE CHOOSE

Imagine two mirrors side by side:
- » **The Carnival Mirror:** Distorted by cultural trends, past failures, and others' opinions
- » **God's Mirror:** Perfectly reflecting who He says you are (James 1:23-24)

Like Michael, a recovering addict who told me, "I saw myself as 'just a junkie' until I read Psalm 139:14 aloud every morning for a year," many of us need help shifting our gaze to the right mirror.

Psalm 139:14 declares, "I praise you because I am fearfully and wonderfully made; your works are wonderful, I know that full well." If I'm being honest, for a long time, I didn't know this "full well." I struggled with believing that I was fearfully and wonderfully made when I felt stuck in a constant cycle of self-doubt and insecurity. How could someone who felt so flawed be God's masterpiece? Maybe you've wondered the same.

This reminds me of a powerful story about a lion that grew up among sheep. The lion, separated from its pride as a cub, was raised by sheep and began to see itself as one of them. It bleated like a sheep, ate like a sheep, and ran in fear every time the lion from the jungle appeared. One day, as the flock was drinking water by a stream, the young lion saw its reflection for the first time. It froze in shock, realizing that its image did not match the sheep around it—it matched the lion that terrified them. That moment of clarity changed everything. When the lion from the jungle appeared again, the young lion didn't run away this time. Instead, it followed the older lion back into the wild, where it learned to embrace its true identity and power.

Like that lion, many of us live our lives believing we are something less than what we truly are because the voices, experiences, and limitations of those around us have shaped us. We forget that our true reflection can only be found in the Word of God. James 1:23-24 compares this to a person who looks into a mirror, sees their face, and then immediately forgets what they look like. But the Word is not just any mirror—it's the ultimate reflection of who we are in Christ. It shows us our true identity as fearfully and wonderfully made children of God, empowered to live with purpose.

STORIES OF TRANSFORMED SIGHT

1) The Lion Who Thought He Was a Sheep

Like the sheep who raised the lion in our opening story, oryx antelopes raised Kamunyak—a real lion cub in Kenya—until rescuers helped her rediscover her true nature. Many of us live as "spiritual oryxes" when we're called to be lions of God's kingdom.

2) From Janitor to Lifesaver

Samuel Harrison, an uneducated hospital janitor, was told he was "just a cleaner." But when doctors discovered his blood contained rare antibodies, he became the "Man with the Golden Arm," donating blood that saved 2.4 million babies from Rhesus disease.

3) The Reluctant Speaker

Jennifer, a timid pastor's wife, avoided public speaking until she claimed 2 Corinthians 3:18: *"We are being transformed into His image.*" Today, she leads a women's ministry, reaching thousands.

Let me ask you, dear reader: When have you sensed God inviting you beyond your self-perceived limits? What "carnival mirror" distortions have you believed about yourself? During my season of deep self-doubt, God whispered: "You are more than what you see. Look through My eyes." When I opened to 2 Corinthians 5:17, "If anyone is in Christ, the new creation has come," it was like the lion seeing his true reflection—the lies began crumbling.

The world will often reflect back to us a distorted image of who we are—telling us we're not good enough, not smart enough, or not worthy of love. But when we look into the stream of God's Word, we see the truth: we are created in His image, called for a purpose, and equipped with gifts that only we can bring to the world. His Word reminds us that we are to be fearless and bold. We've been created to make an impact for His kingdom. The Word reminds us that we are not meant to crawl or cower—we are designed to soar.

> *You are neither bound by your past nor defined by the opinions of others.*

This chapter is your invitation to break free—to unshackle your wings from the lies, limitations, and labels that have kept you grounded. It's time to see yourself as God sees you, to embrace your true identity as an eagle, and to rise above the noise and distractions of the world.

Pause for a moment and look into the mirror of God's Word. What do you see? Not a reflection of fear, doubt, or failure but a reflection of strength, purpose, and destiny. You are neither bound by your past nor defined by the opinions of others. You are God's masterpiece, fearfully and wonderfully made—crafted for greatness, created to soar beyond limits and step boldly into your divine calling.

There was a season in my life that stands out vividly. I found myself at a particularly low point; constant comparison to others and feeling that I could never measure up weighed me down. Despite working hard, pushing myself, and diligently trying to meet every expectation, it always felt like I was falling short. I questioned my progress in every area of my life—my career, finances, ministry, motherhood, marriage, friendships, and even as a sister. No matter how much I accomplished, it never seemed like enough.

One evening, overwhelmed and feeling utterly defeated, I turned to God in prayer. I poured out my heart, sharing every fear, frustration, and inadequacy. In the stillness of that moment, I felt His gentle whisper deep in my spirit: *You are more than what you see. Look at yourself through My eyes.*

> *He doesn't just see your flaws or struggles; He sees your potential, your beauty, and the incredible person He's shaping you to be.*

That simple yet profound message began to shift my perspective. It was a reminder that God sees beyond our perceived shortcomings and limitations. He looks at us with love, purpose, and the fullness of His grace. It was the start of a journey to view myself not through the lens of comparison or self-doubt but through the truth of who I am in Him. As I practice staying quiet before God, I remember a particular moment I opened my Bible. I came across the promise of 2 Corinthians 5:17: "Therefore, if anyone is in Christ, the new creation has come: The old has gone, the new is here!" It felt like looking into the stream, like the lion, and seeing for the first time who God had called me to be. That truth began to strip away the lies I had believed about myself and replace them with the confidence that I was His beloved child.

At first, I wasn't entirely sure what that meant. But as I leaned into His Word and spent more time in prayer, God began to reveal what He meant. He opened my eyes to the truth of my identity—not as someone defined by mistakes, insecurities, or the standards of the world but as someone deeply loved, intentionally created, and equipped with a purpose. It wasn't an overnight transformation, but it was the start of something life-changing. He was inviting me to stop looking at myself through my limited, flawed perspective and instead see myself through the lens of His perfect love.

Think about an eagle soaring high above the earth. From the ground, you might see just a small shadow or a distant silhouette, but from the eagle's perspective, the view is expansive and all-encompassing. In the same way, God sees so much more in you than you can from your earthly vantage point. He doesn't just see your flaws or struggles; He sees your potential, your beauty, and the incredible person He's shaping you to be. He sees the gifts and abilities He's placed in you and the purpose He's created you to fulfill.

I'll never forget another specific moment when this truth became so real to me. I faced a daunting task—a project that felt way beyond my abilities. I doubted myself and almost gave up before I even started. But I felt God prompting me to step out in faith, reminding me that His strength is made perfect in my weakness (2 Corinthians 12:9). As I obeyed and took it one step at a time, I saw Him accomplish far more through me than I could have imagined. That experience was a powerful reminder that when we trust God's perspective, we can overcome even the biggest challenges.

The story of the lion above serves as a powerful metaphor for self-discovery, awakening, and stepping into one's true identity. It teaches us that we often conform to the environment we grow up in, even if it doesn't align with our true nature. There comes a moment of realization (symbolized by the stream and the reflection) where we see ourselves for who we truly are. Embracing our authentic identity requires courage and often involves leaving behind what's familiar to grow into the person we were meant to be.

As you journey through the pages of this book, my heartfelt prayer is that it inspires you to rise above limiting beliefs, societal pressures, and false identities, empowering you to embrace and unlock your true potential—remembering that the world's labels don't define you—even your self-perception falls short. Only in God's Word do you find your true reflection—and His voice never deceives.

> You are not who the world says you are.
> You are not even who you think you are.
> You are who God says you are—
> and His Word is the only mirror that never lies.
> —Tessy Tanyi

CHAPTER 2

THE AWAKENING

Breaking Free from the Cage

There comes a moment in life when something inside you shifts. It's as if the blindfold has been removed, and you suddenly see the reality of your existence. You realize that you've been living below your potential, confined by the limitations of fear, doubt, and the expectations of others. **This is the awakening.** This is not just a revelation—it is a call to action. It is the moment you recognize that God has called you to more, and you refuse to settle for anything less. It is the realization that you were never created to live an ordinary life. It doesn't happen by chance. It happens when you dare to question, to seek, and to rise.

THE SOUND OF AWAKENING IS FOR YOU

It is never too late to awaken to your true potential. Whether you are reading this book in the prime of your youth, still discovering who you are, or are advanced in age, wondering if your time has passed—know this: the call to awaken is for you. God's plans for your life are not bound by time, age, or past mistakes. As long as there is breath in your lungs, there is purpose in your journey. The world may try to convince you that your best days are behind you, that you've missed your moment, or that it's too late to change course—but nothing could be further from the truth.

Many of history's most influential people discovered their purpose later in life, proving that it is never too late to awaken to your potential—as purpose has no age limit. Here are some powerful examples:

- Colonel Sanders launched KFC at sixty-five after multiple career failures.
- Vera Wang became a fashion designer at forty after working in journalism.
- Ray Kroc transformed McDonald's into a global brand at fifty-two.
- Julia Child published her first cookbook at fifty, revolutionizing the culinary world.
- Stan Lee created Marvel's superheroes at thirty-nine, with major success in his forties.
- Samuel L. Jackson got his breakthrough role at forty-six after years of struggle.
- Grandma Moses began painting at seventy-eight, becoming a celebrated artist.
- Morgan Freeman became a Hollywood icon at fifty.
- Henry Ford revolutionized the auto industry at forty-five.
- Laura Ingalls Wilder published Little House on the Prairie at sixty-five.
- Moses was eighty years old when he led the Israelites out of Egypt.
- Abraham became the father of nations when he was one hundred.
- Caleb claimed his mountain at eighty-five.

But, on the other hand . . .
- » David was just a shepherd boy when he was anointed king.
- » Jeremiah was young when God called him to be a prophet.
- » Mary was a teenager when she carried the Savior of the world.

The key takeaway is this: *the awakening is for everyone*. It is for the one who has been complacent for too long, for the one who has settled for less, for the one who has allowed fear, doubt, or distractions to rob them of their divine destiny. And it is also for the one who has been walking faithfully but senses that there is more.

This is your moment. The stirring in your spirit, the longing for more, the hunger for purpose—it is God calling you to awaken. You are not here by accident. You were made for something greater. And now, it is time to rise. Whether you're in your twenties or in your eighties, your greatest achievements may still be ahead. It's never too late to embrace your potential, step into your calling, and soar like the eagle you were created to be. The time to awaken is now!

> *The truth is: the cage is not safe—it is suffocating.*

For years, I was unknowingly imprisoned in a mental and spiritual cage—a cage that the world's expectations, limitations of my environment, and my own lies had built. People who had settled for mediocrity and dared not to dream beyond their circumstances surrounded me. They were content with a small life, afraid to step beyond the familiar. Their conversations were limited, their ambitions restrained, and their vision clouded by what they could see in the natural. I desperately wanted more—more of God, more of life, more of the supernatural dimensions of purpose and abundance. I wanted to break free from the cycle of ordinary living and experience the fullness of the kingdom life that God had prepared for me.

But breaking free would require something radical.

THE COST OF AWAKENING

Many people never awaken because they are unwilling to pay the price. Awakening requires discomfort, courage, and transformation. The first price I had to pay was separation. When you awaken, you will realize that not everyone will understand you.

- » Friends who once celebrated you may suddenly feel uncomfortable around you.
- » Family members may think you are taking your faith "too seriously."
- » Society will pressure you to conform to the norm, to stay inside the cage where it's "safe."

But the truth is: **the cage is not safe—it is suffocating.**

One of the biggest traps that keep people in mediocrity is the desire for acceptance. Many are so afraid of rejection that they choose the comfort of conformity over the pain of transformation.

Jesus Himself experienced this. Even His own family misunderstood Him: "For even his own brothers did not believe in Him" (John 7:5).

If Jesus had waited for the approval of others before walking in His calling, we would not have a Savior today.

What about you? Are you waiting for permission to become who God created you to be?

KNOWING WHO YOU ARE AND WHY YOU ARE HERE

There is nothing more dangerous to the enemy than a person who knows their identity and purpose. One of the reasons Jesus was unstoppable was because He knew exactly who He was and why He was on earth: "For I came down from heaven, not to do mine own will, but the will of him that sent me" (John 6:38, KJV). Because He had clarity, opposition did not intimidate Him. He was not afraid of rejection. The opinions of men did not sway Him. Can the same be said of you? Do you know why you are here? Do you have a sense of divine urgency about your life? Or are you still wandering, waiting for someone else to define you? When you lack clarity, others will easily influence you, but when you know who you are and what you were born to do, nothing and no one can stop you.

For me, the awakening wasn't just a gradual process—it was a supernatural encounter that changed the course of my life. On the night of November 21, 2016, my life took a dramatic turn. That evening started like any other—I went about my usual routine, finishing the day with my family, tucking my children into bed, and preparing for rest. But in the middle of the night, something extraordinary happened. I had a vision—one so vivid and real that I can still feel its impact as I write. In the vision, I found myself

> *When God calls you out of the crowd, He means business.*

sitting in the midst of a large crowd. It was a noisy, aimless gathering—people chatting, lost in trivial conversations.

Then, suddenly, an angel of the Lord appeared. Without saying a word, he reached for my hand and led me away from the crowd. I looked around, but no one else seemed to notice what was happening. We walked for what felt like a long distance, yet it also seemed like mere seconds. Then, we arrived at a high mountain top. The angel turned to me, placed his hands on my head, and anointed me with oil. As he did, he spoke words that shook my very being: "I pull you out from the crowd." The moment he said those words, I woke up. I was trembling—the fire of God burned inside me. My life was no longer the same.

Here's what I learned: when God calls you out of the crowd, He means business. From that moment, my hunger for God intensified. I could no longer remain comfortable in the ordinary. I had to seek Him, to pursue Him, to discover what He was calling me to do. I realized that God was calling me to be a voice—to be a messenger of His truth. This realization terrified me at first. Who was I? I didn't feel qualified. I feared rejection. But then God reminded me: "Before I formed you in the womb I knew you, before you were born I set you apart" (Jeremiah 1:5). He used this scripture to tell me that He does not call the qualified—He qualifies the called.

And He is calling you!

THE AWAKENING IS FOR YOU

Perhaps as you read this, something inside you is stirring. Maybe you have felt stuck—trapped in a cycle of fear, self-doubt, or complacency. Maybe you have sensed God calling you to more, but you've been hesitant to respond. This is your awakening moment. Like the eagle trapped among chickens . . .

You were never meant to live a small life.
You were never meant to blend in with the crowd.
You were never meant to live in a cage of fear.
You were created to soar.
But here's the truth: no one can make the decision for you.
God is calling, but you must answer.

As you read this book, do not rush the process. Absorb every truth, every revelation, and every challenge that this book presents. Let these words sink deep into your spirit. There will be moments when you need to pause—to reflect, to question, to analyze, and to make real commitments that will shift the course of your life. Don't resist those moments. Lean into them. This book is more than just words; it is a roadmap, a guide to your transformation.

Separation is not punishment— it is preparation.

This journey is about more than just information—it is about revelation. This book is about uncovering the version of you that has been buried under doubt, fear, and the expectations of others. The Holy Spirit has orchestrated this message to lead you into self-discovery, healing, and the power of your divine identity. You will not just read about change—you will experience it.

Your next steps on the path to transformation are to:

1) **Separate Yourself**
   - Identify and break free from the people, habits, and mindsets that have kept you trapped in mediocrity.
   - Dare to step away from anything that stifles your growth—because you cannot soar while shackled to the ground.
2) **Seek God's Presence Like Never Before**
   - Prioritize prayer, fasting, and deep study of God's Word like your life depends on it—because it does.
   - Ask Him to reveal His purpose for your life, and listen as He speaks. Your clarity will come in His presence.
3) **Own Your Identity**
   - Stop apologizing for who God has called you to be.
   - Stand boldly in your divine calling, even if it makes others uncomfortable. God's purpose for you is greater than their opinions.
4) **Take Action—NOW!**
   - Do not wait for the "perfect moment."
   - Move before you feel ready, before you have all the answers, and before you see the full picture.
   - Step out in faith. Start walking in your purpose, even if it feels uncomfortable.

The transformation you seek is waiting for your decision—a decision to separate, seek, embrace, and act. So, will you rise? Will you let out your wings and soar? The choice is yours. And your future is waiting because in every generation, God is looking for individuals who are willing to stand out, to be different, and to align themselves fully with His purpose. The path to greatness in the kingdom of God has never been about blending in with the crowd—it has always been about separation. The Bible presents examples of men and women who chose to stand with God and allow the world to judge them rather than stand with the world and allow God to judge them. Their separation from the crowd was not a loss—it was the very password to their destiny, their gateway to extraordinary impact.

The question is: are you willing to stand out?

GOD CALLS AND THEN HE SEPARATES

Whenever God is about to do something significant, revolutionary, and history-defining, He starts by calling out a man or a woman and setting them apart. Look through the pages of Scripture, and you will see this pattern over and over again. Before God used Moses, He separated him from Pharaoh's palace. Before He made Abraham the father of many nations, He told him to leave his country and his family. Before Jesus launched His ministry, He went into the wilderness.

Separation is not punishment—it is preparation. When God is ready to do a new thing on the earth, He searches for a vessel. But before He can fill that vessel with power, He first calls it to holiness, consecration, and distinction. We will explore the wilderness experience in greater depth later in this book. For now, let's briefly examine some key examples of God's call and separation of His chosen vessels.

Noah's Password: Righteousness in a Corrupt Generation

"Noah was a righteous man, blameless among the people of his time, and he walked faithfully with God" (Genesis 6:9). Noah lived in a time of great wickedness. The world was corrupt, evil was rampant, and morality had all but disappeared. Yet, Noah chose to stand alone. While others lived as they pleased, Noah walked faithfully with God. When the world was indulging in sin, Noah built an ark. When others laughed, he obeyed. His separation from the crowd was the key to his preservation and promotion.

Those who stand with God will see the world bow before them. Those who bend their knees to God will never need to bend to men. This is the password of every man and woman who is producing greatness for the Lord today. Will you use it?

Daniel's Password: Resolute Conviction

"But Daniel resolved that he would not defile himself with the king's food, or with the wine that he drank" (Daniel 1:8, ESV). Daniel was taken captive to Babylon—a foreign land hostile to the ways of God. He was given a new name, a new identity, and a new environment. Yet, he refused to conform. When given food that violated God's laws, he resolved not to defile himself. Resolve means to be firmly committed to a principle or purpose. It means to refuse to be swayed, pressured, or manipulated. Daniel's separation from worldly pleasures led to his divine elevation. The same applies today. We live in a world that pressures us to fit in—to compromise our values, to water down our convictions, and to go with the flow. But like Daniel, it is not enough to merely *want* to do God's will. We must resolve to stand firm.

Are you willing to separate yourself?
Are you willing to be ridiculed for your faith?
Are you willing to say no when the world says yes?
Are you willing to choose holiness in a world that embraces sin?

Daniel served for over seventy years in Babylon—a kingdom hostile to God. Yet, he never compromised his faith. He remained truthful when it was dangerous. He remained faithful in prayer when it was illegal. He refused to seek personal glory when power was offered to him. God honored him. He was delivered from death, elevated to high office, and his enemies were silenced. When God makes you, no man can break you. When God elevates you, no man can bring you down. If you stand with unwavering conviction, you will not only survive the test—you will thrive and rise above the rest.

One of the greatest hindrances to spiritual greatness is the need for acceptance. Many believers lose their identity because they are afraid of standing with God—especially if it means standing alone. They choose to blend in because they fear rejection, don't want to be labeled as "too spiritual," or are afraid of persecution. But let me tell you the truth: if you blend in, you will get lost in the crowd. Just as eagles soar alone while chickens huddle together on the ground, you were not created to be ordinary.

If you blend in, you will get lost in the crowd.

Ever notice how marathon runners bond at races, or artists collide in coffee shops? "Birds of a feather flock together" isn't just an observation—it's a call to audit your "flock." Are the people around you lifting you toward your purpose or clipping your wings? Sometimes, growth means leaving the flock to find new altitudes. If you spend your days among chickens, you'll learn to scratch the ground and cluck in fear. But if you soar with eagles, you'll rise above the noise and learn to dominate the skies.

If you spend your time with people who lack vision, soon your dreams will start to shrink.

If you listen to the voices of fear and doubt, soon, you will stop believing in yourself.

That's why God separates His chosen ones.

YOU WERE CREATED TO BE RARE

In economics, value is determined by rarity.
- » Real pearls are costly because they are hard to find.
- » Diamonds are expensive because no two are exactly alike.
- » Gold is valuable because it must be mined and refined.

Likewise, God made you rare.
- » You are not mass-produced.
- » You are not made for the discount rack.
- » You were never meant to blend in.
- » You were created to be a light.
- » You were born to stand out.

You are Designer-made by the Creator Himself. It is never God's intention for any individual to get lost in the midst of everyone else. God created you to stand out. There are over seven billion people on the planet, and not one of them has your fingerprints. Let us examine some aspects of God's creation. There are thousands of kinds of flowers in the world. You may say they are all flowers, but do not forget that each is unique among its species. When you see a forest from a far distance, at first glance, all the trees in the forest seem to blend together. But, as you take a much closer look, you will see that the shape of each tree is unique. You will realize that each type of tree has a distinct design. Why? Uniqueness is part of God's creation.

The world will try to force you to conform, but do not give in. God is calling you to awaken. He is calling you to separate yourself, embrace your true identity, and walk boldly in your purpose.

If you choose to stand with God, the world may resist you for a season, but in the end, it will have no choice but to recognize God's hand on your life. So, rise up. Step into your divine calling. Take your place among the eagles. And soar! Will you accept the call?

THE DREAM THAT CHANGED EVERYTHING

One fateful night, I was thrust into a harrowing dream, my body drenched in sweat as I raced through the darkness. Shadows loomed behind me—demonic forces closing in, their presence suffocating, relentless. My heart pounded like a war drum, each step feeling heavier, as though the very air conspired against my escape. Then, something extraordinary happened—*I heard a voice.*

A voice, powerful yet gentle, pierced through the darkness: *Tessy, let out your wings and soar!*

In that instant, the supernatural unfolded. I felt a shift—my body transformed. My arms stretched into mighty wings, my feet lifted from the ground, and suddenly, I was soaring. The fear that had held me captive vanished. I rose above the chaos, above the relentless pursuit, above the limitations of the earth. The demonic figures that once seemed so overwhelming now shrank beneath me, dwindling into insignificance like tiny ants. The higher I soared, the less they mattered.

When I awoke, my heart still pounding, the Spirit of the Lord whispered to me: *Tessy, you are an eagle. When you soar as you were created to, all your problems become nothing in the presence of My power.*

It was a divine revelation. So many believers today struggle because they are running when they should be soaring. They fight battles on the ground when they are designed to rise above them. The enemy thrives on keeping us bound to earthly limitations, but God has called us higher. The moment we embrace our true identity as kingdom eagles, we shift from striving to soaring—from fear to dominion. This divine revelation was God's way of reaffirming His call for me to take my rightful place—to fully embrace my God-given identity, rise above earthly limitations, and trust in His strength rather than striving in my own. He was showing me that true victory doesn't come from human effort alone but from ascending higher in Him, operating from a place of divine authority rather than merely trying to escape life's battles.

Just as I heard the voice commanding me to soar, I believe that today, as you read this, God is calling you higher. He is saying, "No more merely walking when you were designed to soar; no more settling when I created you to rise above." The sky is not your limit—it's your domain. Now is the time to step into who you were always meant to be.

But here lies the problem—too many believers have forgotten who they truly are. They have exchanged their divine inheritance for a life of comfort and complacency, settling for the barnyard when they were created for the heavens. Chickens remain earthbound, confined to scratching the dirt, never knowing the freedom of the open sky. They live in limitation, always looking down, never realizing they were made for more. But eagles—eagles are limitless! They rise above the storms, they own the skies, and they embrace the boundless life they were created for. Which will you choose? Will you remain in the safety of the familiar, or will you dare to spread your wings and claim the heights God has destined for you? The sky is waiting. Your destiny is calling. It's time to soar!

TIME TO BREAK FREE FROM THE CAGE OF MEDIOCRITY

In the opening chapter, you read an example of what happens when an eagle is raised among chickens. It forgets who it is. It loses sight of its wings, its strength, and its destiny. Instead of soaring, it scratches the ground, believing the lie that it was never meant for more.

How many of you have spent years in an environment that convinced you that you're just like everyone else? You've heard the whispers:

"Don't dream too big."

"Stay in your lane."

"You're not qualified for greater things."

And so, you stopped stretching your wings. You stopped reaching beyond the limits placed on you. You forgot that you were created for something greater.

But today, God is waking you up! In my dream, I could have wished for wings. I could have prayed for strength to keep running. But nothing changed until I obeyed the command to fly. Many believers long to soar, but they refuse to leave the ground. They talk about their dreams but never take action. They wait for a sign, for a push, for the "right time." How about you? What are you waiting for? People's approval? For fear to disappear? Remember: Moses didn't wait for Pharaoh's permission—he led Israel to freedom. David didn't wait until he was older—he ran towards Goliath with a slingshot. It's time to **stop waiting and start soaring.** Your destiny is calling. Step out, spread your wings, and take flight!

Let today be the day you awaken to your true identity and begin to live the life you were always meant to live! You are God's chosen vessel—marked, anointed, and destined for greatness. So, spread your wings, and let yourself soar—higher, farther, and with a purpose that you were born to fulfill.

> Cages are meant for birds, not eagles.
> Chains are made for prisoners, not royalty.
> You've been called to soar—so stop rehearsing captivity and start practicing your wings.
> —Tessy Tanyi

CHAPTER 3

IDENTITY CRISIS

Created for Greatness

In the cool of the evening, the fine summer breeze poured its fresh aroma on the pleasant, dry, and dusty Ellerslie road in the city of Edmonton, Alberta, Canada as I made my way to my humble home in the neighboring street. On my way, the chirping of the birds drew my attention to the cemetery on the left side of the street as I walked by. I have often passed by this cemetery, but for the first time, it piqued my interest. As I turned and took a second look at the low-fenced and wide-opened gates of the cemetery, what I saw were graves holding the intact or cremated remains of dead people. I asked myself: *Who are the people buried or interred in those graves? What type of life did they live here on earth? What did they accomplish? What footprints did they leave for their generations and generations to come? Did they maximize their potential, or did they take it back to the grave? Did they allow the beautiful, majestic eagle of potential to soar, or did they keep it trapped within them while they lived and died like a chicken?*

Tragedy strikes when a tree dies in a seed, a man dies in a boy, a woman dies in a girl, and an eagle dies living like a chicken.

From that moment, I began to reflect deeply on the question: why am I here on this earth?

How about you? Have you ever paused to wonder about your purpose? I've asked myself this question countless times, especially during seasons when life felt stagnant, confusing, or overwhelming. Those moments when it feels like you're just going through the motions—waking up, doing what's expected, and ending the day without a sense of real fulfillment—have often prompted me to ask God, "Is this all there is?"

> *Purpose isn't always about achieving something the world considers monumental—it's often about being obedient in the small things.*

The truth is, you were created with a purpose. God didn't form you randomly or set you adrift without direction. He designed you intentionally, with every detail of your life woven together to fulfill a specific plan. He has equipped you with unique gifts, passions, and experiences that align with His kingdom work. One verse that became a lifeline for me during my moments of uncertainty was Ephesians 2:10: "For we are God's handiwork, created in Christ Jesus to do good works, which God prepared in advance for us to do." This verse was a powerful reminder that I wasn't just existing or trying to survive—God handcrafted me for something meaningful, even if I couldn't fully see what that "something" was just yet.

I used to believe that purpose had to be something grand and dramatic, like leading a global ministry, writing a bestselling book, or making an impact that the whole world could see. But over time, God gently showed me that purpose often unfolds in the small, faithful steps we take every single day. Purpose isn't always about achieving something the world considers monumental—it's often about being obedient in the small things.

For example, I remember a season when I was helping organize community outreach events at church. It seemed like a simple task—planning logistics, coordinating volunteers, and running errands. But one day, a single mom came up to me after an event and shared how much the church's support meant to her. She told me it was the first time in years that she felt seen and cared for. That moment reminded me that even small acts of obedience—like showing up to serve—can carry eternal significance.

> *Purpose doesn't always look like a big, flashing neon sign; sometimes, it's as simple as being faithful in what God has placed before you today.*

Another example came when a friend called me late at night, overwhelmed by a difficult situation. I felt tired and unsure of what to say, but I decided to just listen and pray with her. Months later, she told me that the conversation helped her feel God's peace and gave her the strength to move forward. That taught me that purpose can be as simple as showing up for the people God places in your life.

As I continued to prayerfully seek clarity on my purpose, the Holy Spirit revealed something profound: to truly understand why I am here, I must first understand who I am in Christ. My identity in God is the foundation for everything. I began to realize that my worth isn't tied to achievements or recognition but to the fact that I am a child of God, loved and chosen. Understanding this helped me let go of the pressure to strive for purpose and instead lean into His plans for my life.

Knowing who you are in Christ frees you to embrace both the grand moments and the seemingly small, everyday opportunities to walk in purpose. Whether it's encouraging someone with a kind word, volunteering your time, or simply being present with your family, every act done in obedience to God has value. Purpose doesn't always look like a big, flashing neon sign; sometimes, it's as simple as being faithful in what God has placed before you today. It's in these moments of surrender and trust that God's greater purpose for your life begins to unfold.

Each day, millions of people exit this planet called Earth without realizing who they are; therefore, they never fulfilled all that they are capable of accomplishing. The cemetery down the street in your neighborhood contains authors who never wrote a book, singers who never sang a song, preachers who never shared the gospel, actors who never read any scripts, men and women with wings who never flew, and people who buried their God-given potential under the basement of their destiny because they never really knew who they were.

Often, we die without exploring the gifts, abilities, and successes that are buried within us. This makes the *"What if?"* question a pertinent one at this juncture.

History hinges on identity awakenings:
» *What if Michelangelo* died before touching brush to the ceiling of the Sistine Chapel?
» *What if Moses* never embraced his calling to lead?
» *What if Paul* remained Saul, the persecutor?

Now ask yourself, *What if I die without becoming who God created me to be?*

J. K. Rowling should have fallen victim to death before fulfilling her purpose, but she defied those odds. Before Harry Potter, she was a divorced mother on welfare, and twelve publishers had rejected her. "Failure stripped away the inessential,"[6] she later said. Her crisis became the crucible for a legacy that would inspire millions.

Hear me: *don't die without having truly lived!* Since our God is a limitless God, strive to be all that He has created you to be, to do the things He has sent you here to do, and to go places He has destined for you. Strive to live a life of no limits! Perhaps you are wasting your life doing nothing. You are not junk—you are loaded with God's divine verities, a true belief of fundamental importance. Spread out your wings and fly. You never know how high you may soar.

Think of a time you compared yourself to someone else. How did it make you feel? That discomfort is a divine alarm—you're seeking validation in the wrong mirror.

---

6 Rowling, J.K. "The Fringe Benefits of Failure, and the Importance of Imagination," June 5, 2008. Cambridge, MA [https://news.harvard.edu/gazette/story/2008/06/text-of-j-k-rowling-speech/].

If you stripped away your job, relationships, and achievements—who would remain? You're not your resume. You're God's handiwork (Ephesians 2:10) and fearfully made (Psalm 139:14).

What dream have you buried as "impractical"? That neglected passion isn't dead—it's a dormant seed waiting for your obedience.

THE MANUFACTURER'S MANUAL AND THE GRAVE OF UNLIVED POTENTIAL

We live in a world obsessed with labels. Job titles. Social media bios. Personality tests that box us into four letters. We introduce ourselves by what we do rather than who we are—as if identity were something to assemble from spare parts rather than discover in sacred alignment. But what happens when the labels don't fit? When the roles feel like costumes, or the world's definitions crumble like counterfeit currency? History's most transformative figures faced this moment—none more starkly than the wilderness preacher whose answer to "Who are you?" revolutionized self-definition:

> *Now this is the testimony of John, when the Jews sent priests and Levites from Jerusalem to ask him, "Who are you?" He confessed, and did not deny, but confessed, "I am not the Christ." And they asked him, "What then? Are you Elijah?" He said, "I am not." "Are you the Prophet?" And he answered, "No." So they said to him, "Who are you? We need to give an answer to those who sent us. What do you say about yourself?" —John 1:19-22 (ESV)*

When religious leaders demanded the Baptist declare himself, his refusal to accept their prefabricated categories ("Are you Elijah? The Prophet?") became the ultimate act of self-awareness. He understood that you cannot borrow your purpose from someone else's expectations.

Like a product's maker knows its function, your Creator embedded your design before the first demand for credentials ever came. This is the grave of unlived potential—when we bury our true selves under borrowed definitions. And this is the manual we've ignored too long.

You will never know what you are capable of without first knowing who you are. The question of identity is: who am I? To correctly answer this question, you have to trace yourself back to the One who created you. No one can know the manufacturer of a product more than the one who made it. Fortunately, God has given us the Manufacturer's Manual—the Bible—and this manual explains who we are and what we are capable of.

The sad news is many people try to answer the latter before the former. The majority of people attempt to answer the question of potential without correctly answering the question of identity. Until your true identity is fully established in your heart, you will not be able to fulfill your potential. The question of identity must be conclusively answered before the question of potential can be addressed. You will never know what you are capable of without first knowing who you are.

We go to school to learn all that we can learn to become all that we can in our attempt to discover our potential. But still, it is all a fruitless effort if we do not know who we are before attempting to find out what we can do. We will short-live our lives and take everything locked away within us back to the grave.

This is why the cemetery in your neighborhood is the richest place. The cemetery down your street holds more than bones; it's a museum of might-have-beens.

No matter how great or qualified you may appear to be in your own eyes, the truth is that if you fail to learn who you are, you will never win the race of life, soar in the heavens, or fulfill your divine purpose. For example, if a lizard wants to compete in a race with a cheetah without knowing who he is, the lizard's false identity has capped his potential, even if Usain Bolt is his mentor (the world-renowned greatest sprinter of all time), and he trained in the most equipped gym. If he knew who he was, he could master his place in life, maximize his potential, and win life's battles.

Many people spend all their time and resources trying to accomplish things that haven't been developed in them simply because they see others doing them. Such people will get to the end of their lives and realize they haven't truly lived—they only tried to live someone else's life.

On the other hand, when someone discovers their true identity, it automatically changes the game. It changes the way they think, act, and talk. It wakes them up to make giant strides and leave their footprints in their destiny. God equipped us with the potential to fulfill our destiny, but knowing who we are helps us discover it, extract it, and refine it for God's glory.

Some people will perform activities that are totally distinct from what God has equipped them to do, and thus take their gifts, talents, divine treasures, and untapped potential to the grave. Many will stay busy and do many things, and yet, the surface of their divine destiny will remain unscratched.

THE LAWYER WHO HAD EVERYTHING AND NOTHING

Consider Mark—Harvard Law graduate, firm partner, and penthouse owner. By the world's standards, he had it all, yet each morning, he stared at his reflection and wondered, *Who am I?* It wasn't until he volunteered at a juvenile detention center that he discovered his true passion. "The first time I helped a kid realize his worth," he confessed, "I finally understood mine."

Like Mark, we often chase success only to find ourselves strangers to our own souls. As you embrace the truth that you were created for greatness, you may feel a deep sense of purpose stirring within you. This truth is not just a comforting idea—it is the foundation of your identity. You are a masterpiece, intricately designed with intention and potential, destined to rise above the ordinary and leave a mark on the world. Yet, stepping into that greatness isn't always easy. The world, with its endless comparisons and expectations, can cloud your vision. Past experiences, doubts, and the weight of external labels can make it difficult to fully grasp who you truly are. Many people, despite being destined for more, find themselves trapped in an identity crisis—unsure of their worth, struggling to break free from the limitations placed on them.

But take heart—this is not where your story ends. Recognizing the struggle is the first step toward overcoming it. The noise may be loud, but it is not louder than the voice of truth that resides within you. You were created for greatness, and that truth is your anchor as you navigate the challenges ahead. Remember these three biblical Anchors:

1) **Moses the Stutterer** (Exodus 4:10-12)
    Crisis: "I can't speak well."
    Truth: God qualifies the called.
2) **Rahab the Outcast** (Joshua 2)
    Crisis: "I'm just a prostitute."
    Truth: Your past doesn't disqualify your future.

3) **Peter the Failure** (John 21:15-17)
Crisis: "I denied Jesus three times."
Truth: Grace rewrites your story.

As we turn the page to Chapter 5, we step into the journey of overcoming our identity crisis. Together, we will confront the battles head-on, dismantling the lies that have held you back and uncovering the truth of who you were always meant to be. This journey will require courage, vulnerability, and a willingness to confront the noise that has distorted your sense of self. But know this: you are not alone. So, as you close this chapter, carry this truth with you: you were created for greatness. And now, with that truth as your foundation, let us step boldly into the next chapter of your story. It's time to unshackle your wings, rise above the noise, and soar into the fullness of your identity.

> Greatness isn't a destination—it's your DNA.
> You don't achieve it; you remember it.
> An identity crisis is God's mercy:
> your lies meeting His truth–the collision between who you've believed you are
> and who He says you've always been.
> Let the false self burn.
> Now, go live what God already wrote over you.
> —Tessy Tanyi

CHAPTER 4

UNMASKING IDENTITY THIEVES

Breaking Free from Personal Lies and False Labels

The journey to greatness begins with knowing who you are. But what happens when that knowing is shaken? When the noise of the world drowns out the voice of truth? In this chapter, we will confront the identity crises that hold us back and discover how to reclaim the truth of our identity. The path may not be easy, but it is necessary, for only when we overcome the crisis can we truly soar.

We all battle voices that try to steal our sense of identity. For me, those voices came in the form of fear and comparison. I would scroll through social media, see other people's accomplishments, and feel like I didn't measure up. Maybe your identity thieves are different—shame from past mistakes, doubts about your abilities, the weight of others' expectations or the need to be validated. Whatever they are, they're not from God.

John 10:10 reminds us, "The thief comes only to steal and kill and destroy; I have come that they may have life, and have it to the full." Jesus doesn't want you to live in the shadows of these lies. He wants you to step into the fullness of life that comes from knowing who you are in Him.

There was a season in my life when I fell into the trap of believing that my worth was directly tied to my productivity. If I wasn't checking off boxes, achieving measurable goals, or crossing visible finish lines, I felt like a failure—not just as a person but as a child of God. Every day seemed like a race to accomplish more, and when I fell short, feelings of inadequacy consumed me. It wasn't just about the workload—it was about my identity. I had unknowingly allowed the lie that "You are what you do" to take root in my heart but in His grace, God began to work on my heart. Through quiet moments of prayer and reflection, He gently reminded me of a foundational truth: my worth isn't in what I do but in who I am—His beloved child. It was a humbling realization, but it brought me so much peace. God began to open my eyes to see that He didn't love me for my accomplishments or how productive I was. He loved me simply because I was His.

One breakthrough moment came during a particularly busy season of my life. I was juggling multiple commitments—family, work, ministry, school, and working on establishing and growing multiple businesses—and constantly feeling stretched too thin. One morning, as I

> *The true measure of success is not in how much you accomplish but in your faithfulness to what God has called you to do.*

was journaling and praying, I felt God whisper to my heart, *Be still, and know that I am God* (Psalm 46:10, NKJV). It hit me: I wasn't permitting myself to be still, to hear His voice, or to prioritize the things that truly mattered. I realized I had been so caught up in what I thought I should do that I hadn't stopped to ask God what He wanted me to do.

As I surrendered this over-busyness to Him, I noticed a change. I began to intentionally slow down and focus on hearing clearly from God. It wasn't easy—I still had moments where I felt the pull to do more and please others. But every time I returned to His truth, I found peace. One of the biggest lessons He taught me was that not everything on my to-do list was a God assignment. My own desire to achieve or the expectations of others that weren't aligned with His plan for me drove some of those things. In this newfound stillness, God began to place specific assignments on my heart—things that were directly aligned with His will. One of those assignments was the very book you're holding in your hands. Writing this book was not on my radar or part of my plan, but as I sought God's guidance, He made it clear that this was something He wanted me to do. And as I began the process of writing, I realized just how much I had to share about the lessons He had been teaching me. This journey taught me that God doesn't measure us by the world's standards of success. He values our obedience, our willingness to listen, and our faithfulness to the assignments He places before us. It's not about doing more; it's about doing what He's called us to do. Letting go of the pressure to constantly prove myself and instead embracing His truth has not only freed me from the weight of over-busyness, but it has also allowed me to walk more confidently in the purpose He has for me.

What about you? Have you been caught up in the busyness of life, trying to prove your worth through endless activities and accomplishments? Are you feeling stretched thin or questioning whether you're doing enough? Take a moment to pause and ask God, "What do You want me to focus on today?" Even if the results aren't immediately visible, obeying His guidance brings immeasurable peace and fulfillment. Remember, the true measure of success is not in how much you accomplish but in your faithfulness to what God has called you to do. His plans yield eternal rewards far beyond anything we can imagine. Will you take that step of trust today? Join me on a journey to discover success from God's perspective!

MEASURING SUCCESS, THE RIGHT WAY

In the story of the eagle that lived and dined with the chickens, the eaglet may have been viewed as very successful in terms of size or weight and the largeness of its feathers from the chickens' perspectives. He may have been greatly admired and rated very successful in the eyes of the chickens based on how fast he could eat or hop around the chicken coop. But in the eyes of God, his true Creator, the eagle would be seen as a failure if he never flew or lived the majestic eagle life. Truth must be told. You can be the best lawyer and still not fulfill your destiny, the best doctor and still be trapped in the barnyard of your prophetic destiny, or the best pilot who never flew to the heights that God has called you to soar.

God does not measure success the way man measures success. From the world's viewpoint, success is having a beautiful lake-view home, exotic cars, a diamond necklace, gold wristwatches, designer handbags and shoes, and a vacation home. You name it . . . one can have all these things and still be unsuccessful in the eyes of the

Creator. Success (which is subjective) is the standard of the world, but purpose is the standard of God's kingdom. True success must be measured from God's perspective and not a man-made standard. A truly successful man is a man who walked in the center of God's will, doing all that God asked him to do, with all that God equipped him with to do it. Examples include Jesus, who said, "Behold, I have come to do Your will, O God" (Hebrews 10:9, NKJV), Abraham, who became the father of nations, and the apostle Paul, who said, "I have fought the good fight, I have finished the race, I have kept the faith" (2 Timothy 4:7). What will God say at the end of your sojourn here on earth?

YOU ARE THE SUM TOTAL OF ALL YOUR POTENTIAL

In the Bible, God introduced Himself as "I Am" (Exodus 3:14), but God is so many other things. God is the God of the potential principle. God has many identities, and we come from Him. Thus, He expects us to use for His glory because of how much potential we have. God is our Provider, our Healer, our banner, our Peace, our righteousness . . . the list is endless. In the same manner, His children have no limits. We can be all that He has created us to be and do all that He has called us to do. Our problem is not a money problem or a lack of resources problem—it is a lack of identity problem. It is a failure to recognize who we are and live below God's standards and expectations, imprisoning the person that God created.

At this junction, I want you to embrace the truth that identity isn't found—it's remembered. Your spiritual journey isn't about searching for something you've lost but awakening to what's always been true. Your authentic self isn't hidden like buried treasure waiting to be discovered but rather being revealed like a long-forgotten truth suddenly remembered. Just as the prodigal son "came to himself" (Luke 15:17) before returning home, true transformation begins with this sacred realization. God isn't making you into someone new—He's restoring His original masterpiece, chiseling away the layers of shame, failure, and worldly distortion that have obscured your true design. Your eternal identity was secured at the cross before you took your first breath (Ephesians 1:4), and Christ now serves as the perfect mirror reflecting who you really are (2 Corinthians 3:18). This is why scripture speaks of being "renewed" rather than remade (Colossians 3:10)—we're returning to our pre-fall design, like the psalmist's cry to "return to [our] rest" (Psalm 116:7, author addition). This paradigm shift transforms everything: spiritual growth becomes self-recovery rather than self-improvement, repentance means turning back rather than starting over, and life purpose emerges from discovering God's design rather than deciding our own destiny. Your sins and wounds never defined you—they only distorted the glorious identity that has always been yours in Christ. This was certainly true for Saul: "The Spirit of the LORD will come

> *Your sins and wounds never defined you—they only distorted the glorious identity that has always been yours in Christ.*

powerfully upon you, and you will prophesy with them; and you will be changed into a different person" (1 Samuel 10:5-6).

In this scripture, Saul was told that he would come into the company of prophets, and when he got into their midst, he would become another man. This applies to every one of us today. There is another person on the inside of you that is yet to manifest. I'm referring to your true identity. It's never on the surface, never in plain sight—it lies deep inside you. Truth is, no matter how little or how much you have achieved, how well or how badly you have lived, how fast or how slow you have traveled, there are still many selves within you, just like our Father! Many selves yet to be discovered, that lie dormant, untapped, and unused. As rivers flow from their source, so we carry our Father's limitless nature within us. What God is by eternity, we become by inheritance—His children, unbound by the world's small expectations. Jesus said, "The Son can do nothing of Himself, but what He sees the Father do" (John 5:19). This is the divine principle: children operate in their father's nature. Since our Father is God Almighty, His limitless power and potential become our spiritual inheritance. When I look at my limitations, I hear the Spirit whisper: *You're judging yourself by human standards, but you have a heavenly Father. His nature in you makes the impossible just another family trait.*

YOU CANNOT SPELL "NOTHING" WITHOUT SPELLING "THING"

Rehab was a prostitute but a truly kind woman on the inside. After showing kindness to the Israelite men, she then interceded for her entire family. This means there was an intercessor in the harlot. There was boldness, courage, and beauty trapped in this prostitute.

In Joshua 6:22, Joshua commanded the two men who had spied out the land of Jericho to go into the prostitute's house and bring him the woman. So, there was a woman in this harlot. There's always a thing in nothing. There are great things on the inside of every man and woman that need to manifest. There are divine treasures locked up inside of you. Some gifts and virtues have been locked up for too long. The Bible says there are "treasures in earthen vessels" (2 Corinthians 4:7, NKJV). You are the vessel, and it is time for the treasures inside of you to manifest.

As you read these words, I encourage you to "SET FREE THE TRUE YOU" and get ready to be propelled into your prophetic destiny. Receive the power, wisdom, and grace you need to unleash the treasures bounded by your earthen vessel. Let your divine potential be activated. I call out the strength masked by your weakness. I call out the riches entombed within your lack. I call out the fame from under your shame. I call out the divine appointment cowering behind your terrible disappointments. I call out the wisdom concealed by your foolishness. I provoke the spiritual that is yet to be revealed in your carnal. I activate the divine that is yet to emerge from your mundane.

Saul wasn't born into royalty—he was just an ordinary shepherd's son until he encountered a prophet of the destiny-changing God. That single encounter transformed his life, ushering in a supernatural turnaround. Saul came to the prophet hoping to be told how to locate his father's missing donkey, but after he handed a gift to the prophet, the unexpected happened: he was pulled out of obscurity into a marvelous light. As you read these words, my prayer is that you, too, will experience blessings far greater than those of your fathers and ancestors. May everything needed to activate your divine destiny find its way to you, and may these words infuse your spirit with faith, hope, and the power to step into your God-ordained purpose.

You're not becoming someone new; you're returning to who you always were in Christ:

» **Not** "I'm just a . . ." but "I'm chosen" (see 1 Peter 2:9).
» **Not** "I'm too damaged" but "I'm being made new" (see 2 Corinthians 5:17).
» **Not** "I have nothing to offer" but "I'm equipped for divine purpose" (see Hebrews 13:21).

God expects us to come to the full realization of who we are so that we can live the life He designed, maximize our full potential, and fulfill our prophetic destiny. Often, we die without exploring the gifts, abilities, and successes that are buried within. Remember, there was a giant slayer locked within shepherd boy David.

One day, my seven-year-old son named Jayden came home with a note from his teacher. After reading the contents of the note, which explained that Jaden had a terrible day at school due to issues and distractions that he caused in class, I sat him down and asked him what happened in his classroom. He told me but maintained that he hadn't caused it. He said a student from his class kept bothering him, and he couldn't bear it anymore; he had to retaliate.

I asked him, "Then why didn't you go report him to your teacher?"

> *When you know who you are, it changes the way you talk, think, and act.*

To this, my son replied, "I didn't report it to my teacher because she won't believe me; she thinks I am very bad, and I am the cause of every problem in my class. If she already sees me that way, then why should I bother talking to her?"

His words touched me deeply, so I immediately scheduled an appointment with the teacher. During the appointment, she told me that Jaden had done something similar in the past, so she assumed he was the initiator each time a fight occurred. I told her that she cannot define anyone by their past mistakes or based on her own assumptions. She cannot give him an identity that is not his. She cannot break his wings and expect him to soar. If she does not take care of the minor problems in the classroom, they will grow, and before you know it, the entire school will perceive him differently—as a bully—and no one will like him. This new perception will creep into his mind and cause severe damage to how he sees himself and his perspective on life as a whole.

Millions of people are walking the face of this earth, lost and living life below their standards. They have no sense of who they are, where they come from, or where they are going. When you don't know who you are, a lack of purpose and a mundane life is inevitable. We find some of these people well-dressed in a suit and tie or adorned in fine jewelry, but they still can't find their identity. Every day on the news, we hear about children and young adults who are committing suicide due to false identities. We see the body of Christ fighting, quarreling, and raising all manner of standards against each other because of a lack of identity. Your identity is interwoven in your potential. When you know who you are, it changes the way you talk, think, and act. It changes the way you view yourself, and it empowers you to achieve great things.

The identity of a thing or person can be traced back to its potential, and the potential of a thing can be related to its source (the creator). To correctly identify something, you must trace it back to its source. A seed is traced to a fruit, and a fruit is traced to a tree. To know who we are, we need to trace ourselves back to God—the One from Whom and by Whom we came into this world. It doesn't matter how you feel, what you do, or what people say about you; the only thing that matters is who God says you are. In Him, you can find your worth and identity. One way that God reveals who we are to us is by helping us to discover our potential. Our potential can be traced to who we are, and who we are can be traced to God, our Creator.

> *Our potential can be traced to who we are, and who we are can be traced to God, our Creator.*

The question, "Who am I?" often arises in the hearts of human beings. If I ask you who you are, what would you say? Some of you will say, "I am a lawyer," "I am a doctor," or "I am a teacher," but the truth is that who you are is distinct from what you do. The eagle in the book's introduction was gathering pebbles with the chickens in the barnyard instead of soaring across the sky. Gathering pebbles was what the eagle was doing—but an eagle is who it was. So, you see, identity is the true hidden potential that is expressed in each of us. It is of the utmost importance to first answer, "Whose am I?" before you can answer, "Who am I?"

THE FREEDOM OF KNOWING WHOSE YOU ARE

There's a powerful freedom in knowing that you belong to God. When you truly embrace this, fear begins to fade, and striving ceases. Romans 8:15-16 tells us:

> *The Spirit you received does not make you slaves, so that you live in fear again; rather, the Spirit you received brought about your adoption to sonship. And by him we cry, "Abba, Father." The Spirit Himself testifies with our spirit that we are God's children.*

This verse changed everything for me. Knowing that I could call God *Abba*—Father—and that He sees me as His child gave me a security I had never known. No longer did I have to earn His love or fear losing it. It was mine, simply because I was His. I'll never forget the moment this truth really sank in.

I was walking through a difficult season, feeling alone and uncertain. In prayer, I cried out to God, and for the first time, I felt His deep reassurance: *You are mine. Nothing can change that.* That sense of belonging gave me a peace that carried me through the hardest days.

If you ask me, "Who are you?" here's how I would answer: I am an ambassador for Christ, I am a child of promise, I am a disciple of Christ, I am an heir to the kingdom and joint heir with Christ, I am the church of Christ, I am the redeemed of the Lord, I am an eagle, etc. As we learn the names and titles God has given us in His Word, the eagle stands out to me; thus, we will expound on how we exemplify this majestic bird.

As you stand at the edge of this chapter, take a moment to look back at how far you've come. The journey of overcoming an identity crisis is not a straight path—it's a winding road filled with moments of clarity and confusion, courage and fear, setbacks and breakthroughs. But here you are, still standing, still breathing, and still moving forward. That in itself is a victory.

You've begun to dismantle the lies that once held you captive. You've started to see yourself not through the distorted lens of the world but through the truth of who you really are. This is no small feat. It takes courage to confront the noise, to question the labels, and to choose authenticity over approval. And yet, you've done it. You've taken the first steps toward freedom.

But remember, this is not the end of the journey—it's a new beginning. Overcoming an identity crisis is not about arriving at a perfect version of yourself; it's about embracing the process of becoming. It's about learning to walk in the truth of your identity, even when the noise tries to pull you back.

As you turn the page to the next chapter, carry this truth with you: your past, your mistakes, or the opinions of others do not define you. What defines you is the unshakable truth of who you were created to be, and with that truth as your foundation, you are ready to step into the next phase of your journey—a journey of purpose, passion, and unshackled potential.

The road ahead may not always be easy, but it will be worth it. Because you, dear reader, were never meant to live in the shadows of an identity crisis. You were meant to rise, to soar, and to shine.

So, take a deep breath, steady your heart, and step forward. Your wings are unshackled, and the sky is waiting.

CLOSING CHALLENGE

Now, stand before your mirror and speak this over yourself: *"I am who God says I am. I will live the life He dreamed for me. The world's labels stop here."*

Then, get ready to turn on the light within you—the darkness is waiting for what only you can bring.

> "Hell's labels expire now.
> The Judge has ruled:
> You bear only the name God gave you.
> Now, light a match to every counterfeit identity."
> —Tessy Tanyi

But what fills the space where lies once lived? Your true name awaits. . . .

CHAPTER 5

THE EAGLE WITHIN YOU

Your True Identity

Imagine an eagle, high above the mountains, soaring effortlessly through the vast expanse of the sky. Its wings stretch wide, catching the wind as it glides with purpose and power. The eagle does not struggle to fly; it does not doubt its ability to rise. It simply knows what it was created to do—and it does it with unwavering confidence.

Now, imagine that eagle is you. Deep within you, there is a strength, a potential, a greatness that mirrors the eagle's majestic flight. But for too long, you may have been living like a bird in a cage, unaware of the power within your wings. You've doubted your ability to soar, questioned your worth, and allowed the noise of the world to clip your wings. But no more.

In this chapter, we will uncover the eagle within you—the true identity that has been waiting to take flight.

You were not created to crawl, to hide, or to settle. You were created to soar—to rise above the noise, to see life from a higher perspective, and to live with boldness and clarity. The eagle within you is a symbol of your true identity: strong, free, and destined for greatness.

So, take a moment to close your eyes and picture yourself as that eagle. Feel the wind beneath your wings. Sense the freedom that comes with knowing who you are, and as you open your eyes, know that this is not just a dream—it is your reality waiting to be embraced. Let's begin the journey of unleashing the eagle within you.

During Israel's release from captivity, the prophet Isaiah foretells events that will occur regarding the new heavens and earth, when God's people will be completely restored and all believers will live the tremendous Christian life: "But they that wait upon the LORD shall renew their strength; they shall mount up with wings as eagles; they shall run, and not be weary; and they shall walk, and not faint" (Isaiah 40:31, KJV). God likened every one of us to an eagle because He has given us personality traits that are inherent to that of an eagle.

Several years ago, I did a study of eagles and some of these personality traits and discovered that their qualities reside inside of us, but not many of us are willing to discover, activate, and use them to triumph and fulfill our prophetic destiny. Independent of your height, weight, race, and color, you must have the right understanding of life's essentials. You are an earthen vessel holding treasures.

> *Eyes that look are common, but eyes that see are rare.*

The Spirit of God is longing to use you, and for Him to do that, you must be a willing vessel. You must long to know Jesus and the power of His resurrection, to be conformed to His death and, somehow, attain unending life (Philippians 3:10). In this chapter, I will give you some of the main qualities and traits of the eagle. Then, all through the remaining pages of this book, I will show you how their attributes perfectly correlate with what God has lined up inside of you. I hope this will help you to rediscover your true identity and God's predetermined purpose for your life and destiny.

EAGLE TRAITS AND THE SUPERNATURAL CHRISTIAN LIFE

The eagle isn't just a bird—it's heaven's object lesson for supernatural living. Scripture doesn't casually mention this regal creature (Isaiah 40:31)—it spotlights it as God's chosen metaphor for victorious believers. But here's what most miss: every biological trait of this king of birds is a download from heaven, waiting to be activated in your spirit. When God wanted to depict transcendent strength, He bypassed lions and bears to showcase the eagle. Why? Because while others fight earthly battles, eagles live by higher laws—and so do you. Their very design whispers secrets about your spiritual DNA. Now, let's decode the first kingdom principle written into their feathers—The Seeing Eyes of the Eagle—because your vision is about to shift from human to heavenly.

The Seeing Eyes of the Eagle

When God wanted to depict renewed strength, He didn't point to lions or bears—He chose the eagle (Isaiah 40:31). Why? Because every physical trait of this king of birds mirrors a spiritual reality available to believers. Consider first its legendary vision.

The eagle has two sets of eyes, which make her vision very profound—the natural eyes in her resting mode and the second set of eyes that enable her to soar during the storm without damaging her natural eyes. As Christians, we also have two sets of eyes: our natural eyes, which we use to see the natural world around us, and the eyes of our heart, which enable us to see through God's eyes. It grieves my heart to know that the spiritual eyes have become dormant in a majority of so-called believers who choose to see with only their natural eyes. Eyes that look are common, but eyes that see are rare. Our natural eyes see situations, setbacks, limitations, and circumstances, but the eyes of our hearts enable us to see beyond the physical and celebrate opportunities that only the inner eyes can see. Faith calls the things that are not as though they were.

The Projectile Life of The Eagle

Eagles are known to soar to heights that no other birds can. A flying eagle can reach speeds of about seventy-five miles (120 km) per hour. When going long distances or just moving around their territory, they tend to soar twenty to thirty miles (30–50 km) an hour. They are not afraid of the storm; in fact, they use the wind's current to soar higher with little or no effort, as they rely on the wind's thermals. In the same way, God expects believers to rely on the strength of the Holy Spirit to help them sail through the storms of life as they release themselves and become yielded vessels.

The Victorious Life of the Eagle

Another outstanding trait I discovered about the eagle is that they are extremely bold, courageous, and powerful, with the power to lift four to five pounds. They have been seen engaging in battles with the world's most dangerous and poisonous snakes and tearing snake heads off with their beak. When eagles are faced with major storms, they do not fret or look for where to hide like other birds do, but they face the storms head-on and never allow the storms to plague them. The Bible tells us that God has equipped us with this same boldness, courage, and power, like our Lord Jesus Christ told us in Acts 1:8 (AMP): "But you will receive power and ability when the Holy Spirit comes upon you; and you will be My witnesses [to tell people about Me] both in Jerusalem and in all Judea, and Samaria, and even to the ends of the earth."

The prayer for the postmodern churches should no longer be, "Lord, give us power." Instead of praying to God for power, God is looking down upon you and saying, "If only you knew the power that you carry in the womb of your stomach, you would rise up and start acting." Reinhard Bonnke said that God does not sit with the seaters; He moves with the movers. What Christians need is not more power but deep revelation of who they are in Christ. As you read this book, the Spirit is saying to you today that you have been equipped with power and authority from on High to fulfill your divine purpose here on earth.

The Holy Spirit does not come in pieces.

A lady once came to me and said, "Sister Tessy, a powerful woman of God is coming to town; I would like for you to chase after her wherever she goes so that some of her anointing can fall upon you." I looked at her straight in the eyeballs and said to her, "My own anointing doesn't come from chasing after men—but God. If you want me to serve the minister selflessly, for the sole purpose of working for God, that is absolutely fine by me. I love chasing God and serving men. However, if the primary reason for serving this minister becomes targeted toward hope or a hidden agenda to receive some drops of anointing, you may as well count me out or go find someone else who is looking for double, triple, or quadruple portions of anointing." My goal has never been to run after any human being for drops of anointing. My goal has been—and will always be—to syncopate my heart with the Holy Spirit and let Him make His home in me.

The Exploiting Life of the Eagle

The Holy Spirit is the Power Giver, and He lives in the hearts of Christians. He was not given to you to only speak in tongues nor have some spiritual picnics and chat about the revelations you received in dreams or visions. He wants you to work and move in His power. Some Christians have read in the Bible how several folks brought their sick and afflicted ones so that the apostle Peter's shadow would heal them. They also learned that the apostle Paul's aprons and handkerchiefs produced healing and deliverance when laid on the sick. So, because of this, they were desperate for a double portion of the anointing that would enable them to minister like these apostles. You can do the same thing if you know the power currently slumbering inside of you. The anointing on those materials was not a special portion that came from heaven—it was already in Paul. What Paul did was impart the anointing into those aprons and handkerchiefs.

The Holy Spirit does not come in pieces. I have heard some people say, "Holy Spirit, please give me more of You." And I weep and pray to God to enlighten their eyes of understanding. Like the psalmist prayed: "Open my eyes [to spiritual truth] so that I may behold Wonderful things from Your law" (Psalm 119:18, AMP). The Holy Spirit's intention is not to give you one leg today and one hand tomorrow and then one eye in the future once you impress Him. When you received the infilling of the Holy Spirit, He came to live in you without measure. You are a tabernacle of His divine presence. You are a carrier of His verities. Your responsibility is to carry this consciousness, empty yourself of every fleshly thing, and be in constant sync with the Holy Spirit that is in you.

The difference between the prophets of old and us is that the prophets had the Holy Spirit visitation, but we have the Holy Spirit inhabitation. Jesus had this inhabitation, which is why we can do the same works that He did, and even greater according to His promise (John 14:12). The Spirit came upon Jesus to live in and enable Him to do the works of God. The Holy Spirit came upon you that He might live in you—and He is in you right now: "For He whom God has sent speaks the words of God [proclaiming the Father's own message]; for God gives the [gift of the] Spirit without measure [generously and boundlessly]!" (John 3:34, AMP)

It does not matter how many prophets lay their hands on you—though they may impart the presence of the Holy Spirit through the laying on of hands—unless you make your own personal contact with the person of the Holy Spirit, yield yourself to Him, and walk according to His power with the courage and boldness at work in you, that impartation will not last long. You will search for another to lay hands. Like the eagle, you need to unleash that which is on the inside and begin to birth your miracles without fear but with boldness, courage, and confidence in the power of the Holy Spirit. The eagle is not afraid of man, snake, or beast. The Bible tells us that we should not be afraid of the agents of the antichrist (which means the power at work) because He who is in us is far greater than he (Satan) who is in the world (1 John 4:4). David proved this when he knocked down Goliath with one stone—*that* is the power of the Holy Ghost.

The Exclusive Identity of the Eagle

Everybody wants to be somebody, but nobody wants to take a step to become that "dream" person. We live in a century where one of the world's greatest problems stems from lost identity. Too many people are struggling with recognizing who they truly are, while others who have managed to recognize it are drenched with fear of embracing it.

Another reason God likened us to the eagle is the fact that eagles do not mingle with the crowd. They either fly alone or with other eagles but only on occasion. Some may call this pride, but I call it nature.

By nature, the eagle knows who he is; he can swiftly recognize smaller birds and would never succumb to their realm—no matter what. The majority of people have chosen to go through the motions of life. They blend in with what they see as the "norms" and live a lifestyle everyone else—their parents, social circle, people in their church—has pre-defined. What happens? They make the same mundane choices that everyone else makes. The greatest problem in the world is everyone trying to live a life that someone else has already lived.

> *The greatest problem in the world is everyone trying to live a life that someone else has already lived.*

Only a few people are willing to rise up above the bottom realm, soar into the supernatural, and let the world hear their unique voices.

The Mountain Top Life of the Eagle

Some argue that extremism is a breeding ground for fanaticism. However, when it comes to spiritual things and the journey with Jesus Christ into your divine destiny, you can never be too extreme or go too far. The danger actually lies in settling for surface-level experience with God. God's intention is for us to burn hot with heaven's fire. He does not entertain lukewarmness. Those who have excelled in diverse vocations go all the way in and give themselves completely to what they believe in. Authentic Christianity embodies power and glory and excellence and virtue as exemplified in the eagle's nature. The eagle does not nest or hop around on the ground like the chickens. Most of the time, he is found nesting on the mountaintops.

God's greatest desire is for us to quit the monotonous surface-level life and enter into deeper heights where we begin to operate from the Spirit realm. This higher realm is where the Spirit takes over so that you desist from living a life of struggle and fruitless activities with the crowded and competitive bottom riders. The key reason there is so much competition and activity at the bottom is because it is too crowded. Too many people are struggling for scarce resources at the bottom of the pyramid, while there are enormous amounts of untapped and unused resources at the top. This leaves more room and less competition at the top. Never in recorded history has there been an aircraft collision in the sky, but countless numbers of collisions have been reported among vehicles traveling on the roads. You know why—because everyone in that realm is fighting for traveling space. This is also true of your life.

You can never make history traveling at the bottom, but life will beat you down as you experience lots of accidents and close calls. The majestic, flying eagle shows us how to live supernaturally:

There be three things which are too wonderful for me, yea, four which I know not: The way of an eagle in the air; the way of a serpent upon a rock; the way of a ship in the midst of the sea; and the way of a man with a maid.
—Proverbs 30:18-19 (KJV)

The eagle in the sky reveals the mystery of a Christian who has learned to soar in the heavenlies, far above the winds of adversity and storms of life without any visible human means of aid or support. He has learned to partake of the divine nature and now represents God in the way he thinks, talks, and acts.

FROM HESITATION TO SOARING

In our faith journey, we often find ourselves at different stages of growth and confidence. Some of us may feel like we're soaring high, embracing challenges, and boldly living out our faith. Others might feel they are on ground level, perhaps hesitant or uncertain about stepping out of their comfort zones. These different experiences are natural parts of our spiritual walk. They're not about judgment or categorization but rather about recognizing where we are and where we might aspire to be. As we explore this chapter, we'll look at various characteristics that can help us grow in our faith and live out the potential God gave us more fully. I hope that by the end of this chapter, you'll have a clearer picture of your current spiritual state and feel inspired to embrace new heights in your faith journey.

Remember, this is a personal journey, and only you can decide the path you want to take. As Jesus said:

> "In my Father's house are many rooms. If it were not so, would I have told you that I go to prepare a place for you? And if I go and prepare a place for you, I will come again and will take you to myself, that where I am you may be also." —John 14:2-3 (ESV)

This reminds us that God has a place for each of us, and He invites us to a life of growth and closeness with Him. Wherever you find yourself today, know that there's always room for growth, always an invitation to soar higher in your faith. Let's explore together how we can embrace the fullness of life that God intends for us to live.

WHO IS A GROUNDED CHRISTIAN?

To understand this concept, let's reflect on the life of a chicken.

Chickens are fascinating creatures—they have wings, yet they rarely fly. Instead, they remain grounded, scratching the surface for sustenance and staying within familiar boundaries. Similarly, some believers may find themselves living below their God-given potential, never fully embracing the abundant life that Christ offers. This isn't about condemnation but about recognizing untapped potential. As children of God, we all carry divine treasures within us—unique gifts and abilities meant to glorify Him and bless others. Sadly, many of us leave these treasures buried, never discovering or using them to their fullest extent.

Just as chickens are often kept in coops for their protection, we, too, can find that our comfort zones, fears, or societal expectations confine us. These "coops" might feel safe, but they can limit our growth and prevent us from experiencing the fullness of life God would have us live. We might, sometimes, feel like "local champions" along our journey—content with small victories and familiar territories. While there's nothing wrong with being grounded in our local communities, God often calls us to expand our horizons and impact beyond our immediate surroundings. Just as there are diverse breeds of chickens, each of us has unique gifts and callings. However, our purpose extends far beyond mere survival or conformity. We're called to thrive and make a lasting impact, not just "get by" day to day.

> *Our purpose extends far beyond mere survival or conformity.*

In our information-rich world, it's crucial to be discerning about what we feed our minds and spirits. Just as chickens might peck at anything on the ground, we can fall into the habit of consuming any information that comes our way. As children of God, we're called to be more intentional. We should seek nourishment that aligns with God's truth and promotes our spiritual growth. This means being selective about the voices we listen to, the media we consume, and the company we keep. Ask yourself: What am I feeding my spirit? Are the inputs in my life leading me closer to God's purpose for me?

NOURISHING YOUR SPIRIT WISELY

Remember, you were born with greatness within you. Your task is to look inward, discover your true identity in Christ, and courageously step into that reality. As Ephesians 2:10 says, "For we are God's handiwork, created in Christ Jesus to do good works, which God prepared in advance for us to do." As the scripture suggests, God has placed incredible potential within each of us. Instead of settling for a life of unfulfilled possibilities, let's soar higher and live out the purpose God has designed for us. My prayer echoes this sentiment:

Lord,
May I not go to the grave full of unused treasures. Help me discover and use all You have placed within me for Your glory.

Wherever you are on your journey today, remember that God sees your potential and invites you to rise above limitations. You are called to soar higher than you might imagine. Don't let the confines of comfort, the allure of being a "local champion," or indiscriminate spiritual consumption hold you back. Embrace the greatness God has placed within you and step boldly into your divine purpose.

> You are not becoming an eagle—
> you always were one.
> This chapter didn't give you wings;
> it simply reminded you
> they were there all along.
> You didn't grow wings in these pages—
> you discovered the ones God knit into you
> before you took your first breath
> Now, stop practicing the ground.
> The sky has been waiting for its eagle.
> —Tessy Tanyi

CHAPTER 6

REFLECT AND RISE

*The Path Upward Begins
with Looking Inward*

I've often heard that growth is rooted in self-awareness. Every revolution begins with revelation. "The Path Upward Begins with Looking Inward" whispers an ancient secret: the bravest step toward soaring isn't a leap but a look—into the mirror of your soul. Here, in the quiet honesty of reflection, wings are forged. By turning the gaze inward—confronting truths, honoring scars, and reclaiming purpose—we lay the foundation for ascent. Like a climber studying the terrain before scaling a peak, this phrase reminds us that growth isn't about rushing forward but rooting deep, inviting you to pause, reflect, and then rise with intention.

Life is not a series of random events; rather, it is a story that is meticulously woven with intention, meaning, and purpose. Indeed, you, my beloved reader, are the author of your story. The truths you embrace, the dreams you pursue, and the choices you make influence the story of your life. However, to write a story worth living, it is necessary to first pause, reflect, and rise.

Reflection is not about becoming engrossed in regret or ruminating on the past. It is about achieving clarity, learning from your experiences, and aligning your heart with the truth of your identity. Rising is not about pursuing perfection or another individual's definition of success. It involves leading a life that reflects the greatness within you, embracing your unique purpose, and stepping into the fullness of your identity.

One of the most striking examples of reflection and self-examination comes from Nelson Mandela during his twenty-seven years in prison, especially his time on Robben Island. Mandela entered prison a fiery revolutionary, deeply committed to armed resistance against apartheid. But the long years of solitude, hard labor, and isolation forced him into deep reflection. He journaled often, read voraciously, and engaged in introspective thinking about the nature of power, leadership, forgiveness, and the future of South Africa.

> *This is not just about dreaming of a better life—it's about taking intentional steps to create it.*

Through that process, he came to believe that true leadership required understanding, empathy, and the courage to forgive. It was during this period that he developed the philosophy that would eventually guide South Africa through a peaceful transition from apartheid to democracy.

In his autobiography, *Long Walk to Freedom,* Mandela wrote: "As I walked out the door toward the gate that would lead to my freedom,

I knew if I didn't leave my bitterness and hatred behind, I'd still be in prison."⁷ This statement perfectly encapsulates the transformative power of self-examination—how it helped him grow from a militant leader to a symbol of peace and reconciliation.

In this chapter, we will explore the power of reflection and the courage it takes to rise. Together, we will uncover how to look back without fear, look within without judgment, and look forward with hope. This is not just about dreaming of a better life—it's about taking intentional steps to create it.

You were not intended to lead a mundane, ordinary life. You were intended to triumph—to embrace the challenges, celebrate the victories, and live with a sense of purpose that transcends the noise of the world. So, take a deep breath, open your heart, and let's begin the journey of reflecting on where you've been, rising to who you are, and embracing the life you were created for.

PAUSE AND TAKE INVENTORY

Life moves quickly, and without intentional pauses, we risk missing the truth of where we truly stand. Reflection is the sacred space between where you are and who you're called to be. Ask yourself with raw honesty: Does my daily life reflect the identity God has given me, or have I unknowingly settled for less? Notice the habits, thoughts, and choices that align with eagles—soaring with divine purpose—and those that resemble chickens, scratching the same patch of dirt. This isn't about condemnation but clarity. Lamentations 3:22-23 reminds us that God's mercies are new every morning, which means every moment offers a chance to see ourselves as He

---

7 Nelson Mandela, *Long Walk to Freedom: The Autobiography of Nelson Mandela* (New York, NY: Back Bay Books, 1995).

sees us. Before you can rise, you must first reckon with reality. What do your current patterns reveal about your beliefs, fears, or unhealed places?

BREAKING FREE FROM MUNDANITY

Routine can be a comfort or a cage. Reflection disrupts autopilot. Consider: when did "getting by" become enough? Chickens repeat the same cycles—eat, lay eggs, repeat—until their purpose is reduced to utility. But you are not a creature of habit; you are a creation of destiny. The tragedy isn't just settling for mundanity; it's failing to notice you've settled. Take time to examine: What routines have you normalized that dull your spiritual hunger? Where have you traded passion for predictability? This isn't about judging your past but awakening to your present. The overcrowded life of convenience often whispers, "This is fine," while God whispers, "There's more."

Greatness begins with a question: What am I really afraid of? Reflection exposes the gap between "safe" and "surrendered." Jeremiah 29:11 isn't just a promise; it's a mirror. Hold your current life up to it. What do you see? Courage isn't the absence of fear—it's the willingness to name it. Sit with this: What sacrifices have you avoided because comfort felt kinder than calling? Where has "good enough" become the enemy of "God's best"? True reflection isn't passive; it's the soil where obedience takes root. The hard things God calls you to will always require staring down your doubts first.

It's time to leave behind a "run-of-the-mill" lifestyle and embrace the abundant life Jesus promised (John 10:10). Start dreaming again. Start believing again. Start living again. You were created for more than just to survive—you were created to thrive! Take this moment to reflect:

» Are there areas in your life where you've settled for less than God's best?

» What steps can you take today to rise above mediocrity and pursue your divine purpose?

Remember, it's never too late with God. The mundane life may be overpopulated, but the life of greatness is wide open—for those who are willing to rise above and answer His call. Will you step into it?

THE COST OF PRIDE AND THE POWER OF REFLECTION

It's often said—half-jokingly—that some people would rather drive in circles for hours than stop and ask for directions. While lighthearted on the surface, this simple observation reveals a profound truth about human nature: we often resist admitting when we're lost, confused, or in need of help. Whether out of pride, fear of appearing weak, or a desire to maintain control, many of us would rather press on blindly than pause to reflect or seek guidance.

Scripture echoes this sentiment with striking clarity in Ecclesiastes 10:15 (NKJV): "The labor of fools wearies them, For they do not even know how to go to the city!"

This verse highlights the weariness and futility that results from stubbornly persisting in ignorance. Rather than acknowledging our limitations and asking for direction—whether from God, others, or through honest self-examination—we often double down on flawed efforts. True wisdom, however, begins when we humble ourselves enough to reflect, ask, and grow.

A compelling modern example is the story of Sara Blakely, the founder of Spanx, who started her billion-dollar company with just $5,000 and no background in fashion, business, or retail. When she first came up with the idea for footless pantyhose, she spent countless nights reflecting on what women needed—and, more importantly, why existing solutions didn't work. Instead of pretending to know it all, she became a student of the process. She read books, asked endless questions, cold-called factories, and took rejection after rejection as a chance to rethink and refine her approach.

Sara attributes much of her mindset around growth to one simple but powerful lesson from her childhood. Her father would regularly ask her and her brother, "What did you fail at this week?" And if they didn't have an answer, he'd be disappointed—not because they failed but because it meant they weren't trying anything new.

"It changed my mindset completely—failure became about learning and growth, not defeat," she shared in an interview.[8]

That mindset became the fuel behind her billion-dollar success story. By reframing failure as feedback, she unlocked a level of courage and creativity that many people never dare to tap into. Her success wasn't born from pride or overconfidence but

> *Just as humility fuels clarity and direction in our goals, it also unlocks extraordinary power in our relationship with God.*

---

[8] "How I Built This Podcast," *Wondery*, wondery.com/links/how-i-built-this.

from a willingness to examine, adjust, and keep moving forward with humility and purpose. Her journey reminds us that when we stop and reflect—even when it feels uncomfortable—we open the door to creativity, clarity, and incredible breakthroughs.

In short, Sara Blakely has transitioned from building a product empire to empowering others—especially women—to build their own. She continues to promote the power of failure, reflection, humor, and authenticity—a message she regularly shares through her public speaking, interviews, and social media presence.

Sara Blakely's journey reminds us that success often begins not with bold declarations but with quiet self-awareness. Her willingness to reflect, to admit what she didn't know, and to seek help rather than pretend she had all the answers became the foundation of her breakthrough. It was humility—not pride—that opened the door to innovation, resilience, and lasting impact. But this principle extends far beyond business or personal growth—it's a spiritual truth as well. Just as humility fuels clarity and direction in our goals, it also unlocks extraordinary power in our relationship with God.

Failure isn't a sign you're off track—it's often the clearest signal that you're stretching, growing, and daring to do more. When you stop fearing failure and start learning from it, you unlock your potential and move forward with freedom and resilience. Failure, when embraced with the right mindset, can be the very ground where resilience, clarity, and purpose take root. Sara Blakely turned rejection and uncertainty into fuel for innovation by learning to see failure not as an ending but as instruction. And what she discovered in business, John Knox lived out in the spiritual realm.

Knox, a spiritual giant of the Reformation, embodied this same truth in his life of prayer. His approach wasn't rooted in self-assurance or public acclaim but in deep self-examination and a profound sense of dependence on God. In 1566, he prayed: "Thou hast sealed into my heart remission of my sins, which I acknowledge and confess myself to have received by the precious blood of Jesus Christ once shed."[9]

This heartfelt confession reveals the bedrock of his ministry—not a belief in his own strength but an unshakable trust in God's grace. Knox openly admitted, "I have rather need of all than that any hath need of me."[10] This raw humility drove him to his knees—not as a last resort but as his first response. His power didn't come from influence—it came from prayer.

Scripture affirms this in James 5:16 (NLT): "The earnest prayer of a righteous person has great power and produces wonderful results."

Knox's legacy teaches us that when humility meets fervent prayer, the result is spiritual firepower that changes lives and shapes history.

Though they lived in vastly different times and walked completely different paths, Sara Blakely and John Knox demonstrate the same core truth: our greatest power comes not from pretending we have it all together but from acknowledging where we don't. One turned failure into a launchpad for a billion-dollar business. The other turned confession and weakness into a channel for world-shaking prayer.

The bridge between them? Humility. Blakely's willingness to learn from failure led to innovation. Knox's willingness to bow in prayer led to spiritual authority. Both refused to let pride or fear

---

9 John Knox cited in Wayne Sparkman, *This Day in Presbyterian History*, 2 Jan. 2021, https://thisday.pcahistory.org/2021/01/january-3-john-knoxs-anchor/.
10 John Knox cited in Thomas Eglinton, *John Knox: A Man of Prayer*, 31 March 2022, https://ap.org.au/2022/03/31/john-knox-a-man-of-prayer/.

stop them from growing—and in doing so, they impacted lives far beyond their own.

You don't need perfect conditions, flawless credentials, or unshakable confidence to make a difference. What you need is the courage to reflect, the humility to grow, and the faith to keep going—even when it feels like you're failing.

Whether you're building a business, navigating a personal struggle, or seeking deeper spiritual connection, the path forward often begins with the same step: humility. It takes courage to admit you don't have all the answers. But that very admission is what creates space for wisdom, clarity, and divine strength to step in.

If you feel overwhelmed, uncertain, or unqualified, you're in good company. That awareness isn't your weakness—it's your greatest strength. Let it drive you to reflect, to ask, to pray, and to move forward not in your own power but in the power that comes from humility and faith.

Pause. Reflect. Ask for direction. Then, take the next step boldly—because you don't have to walk it alone.

True greatness isn't about perfection; it's about surrender. Whether it's learning from failure in the natural or leaning into God's strength in the spiritual, transformation begins with humility. We grow not by pretending to have all the answers but by bringing our questions, our weaknesses, and our limitations to the One who does.

As believers, we're called to recognize and pursue the greatness God has placed within us—not through pride but through dependence on Him. John Knox embodied this truth. His commitment to obey God rather than seek the approval of others was unwavering. He once said, "I am not master of myself but must obey Him who commands me to speak plain and to flatter no flesh upon the face of the earth."[11]

This resolve to fear God rather than man gave him the boldness to live authentically and the courage to walk in his calling without compromise. His life teaches us that humble dependence on God and bold obedience are not opposites—they are partners. When we acknowledge our weaknesses and seek God's guidance through prayer, we position ourselves to receive His power and fulfill His purpose.

Like Sara Blakely reframing failure as growth and Knox embracing weakness as a path to spiritual authority, we, too, are invited into a rhythm of honest self-examination and courageous action. It is in the tension between humility and boldness that our calling is awakened. And as we live in reverence of God rather than fear of man, we step fully into the greatness He has already prepared for us.

THE INNER JOURNEY TO GREATNESS

Take a moment to look inward. Where in your life have you been circling the same challenges instead of stopping to ask for help, reflect, or pray? What might shift if you chose humility over pride in that area today? Each of us carries the seeds of greatness within but realizing that potential doesn't happen by accident. It requires humility to reflect, faith to surrender, and the courage to take consistent steps forward—even when the path is unclear.

To be committed to your God-given greatness is to recognize that your purpose isn't about applause or approval—it's about obedience. John Knox understood this well. His life was marked by unshakable

---

11 John Knox cited by Dan Graves, *Christian History Institute*, https://christianhistoryinstitute.org/study/module/knox.

dedication to God's calling, even when it meant standing alone. He lived with the deep awareness that his mission wasn't his own but a divine assignment—one that required boldness, clarity, and the resolve to never compromise.

God has placed extraordinary potential within each of us, yet many fail to uncover it because they remain confined by self-doubt, societal expectations, or fear of failure. The greatest surprise in life isn't what the world has to offer—it's what you discover you're capable of when you stop holding back. Thomas Edison once remarked, "If we did all the things we were capable of doing, we would literally astound ourselves."[12] The journey to greatness begins with self-discovery—peeling back the layers of doubt and reconnecting with the authentic self that God created you to be. This process requires intentionality. You must actively seek out your hidden talents, nurture them, and transform them into reality.

> *Talent without discipline burns out. But character endures.*

It's tempting to believe that success belongs to the naturally gifted—the ones born with extraordinary intellect, talent, or charisma. But the truth is, raw ability is only the starting line, not the finish line. What truly separates high achievers from the rest isn't their genius—it's their grit, their habits, and the systems they build to sustain growth.

People who consistently show up, stay humble, and keep learning—even after failure—tend to go farther than those who

---

12 Thomas Edison cited in Carol Moehrle, *Astound Yourself,* The Daily Café, https://www.thedailycafe.com/content/astound-yourself.

rely only on natural talent. Why? Because talent without discipline burns out. But character endures. It's the inner drive to get up again, to ask better questions, to stay teachable, and to grow through discomfort.

Even the most motivated person can't thrive in chaos. Success is rarely the result of one big breakthrough—it's the product of small, daily choices, supported by routines, accountability, and structure. Systems help automate progress. They reduce the mental friction that slows us down and turn growth into a rhythm, not a random spark. You don't need to be extraordinary to start—you just need the courage to build the right habits and the patience to let them compound. The greats weren't born ahead—they built themselves ahead.

Knox's life reminds us that greatness begins not with loud declarations but with quiet decisions to trust, obey, and grow—no matter the cost. And that journey always starts with a simple question: am I willing to be honest with myself?

THE POWER OF COMMITMENT

That kind of obedience—rooted in humility and surrendered purpose—naturally calls us into a life of consistency and discipline. Committing to greatness means embracing consistency and discipline. It's not about achieving perfection overnight but making small, deliberate changes every day that align with God's purpose for your life. This commitment involves:

- » **Setting clear goals:** Define what greatness looks like for you in alignment with God's calling.
- » **Taking responsibility:** Own your actions and decisions without blaming external factors.

- » **Persevering through challenges:** View setbacks as opportunities for growth rather than obstacles.
- » **Prioritizing purpose over convenience:** Understand that pursuing greatness often requires sacrifice and hard work.

When you fully commit to your own growth and greatness, something powerful happens—you naturally begin to inspire others to do the same. People are drawn to those who not only believe in themselves but also see the potential in others and call it out. By boldly living out your purpose, you create a ripple effect. You become a mirror that reflects what's possible. In choosing to rise, you make space for others to rise with you. That's the quiet power of leadership: not forcing others forward but becoming someone who makes them believe they can.

Who in your life might be waiting for permission to grow—just by watching you do it first? What would it look like for you to live boldly in a way that inspires others to rise with you?

LIVING FOR AN AUDIENCE OF ONE

True greatness comes from living for God rather than seeking approval from others. Like John Knox, commit yourself to fearing God above all else: "I have committed to living my entire life afraid of God and not of men." When you align your life with kingdom realities rather than worldly opinions, you free yourself from the constraints of people-pleasing and step fully into the life God has called you to live.

As we conclude this chapter, remember that greatness is not reserved for a select few—it is available to anyone willing to commit themselves fully to their God-given purpose. This journey requires humility, self-awareness, discipline, and faith. As you embrace this call, remember that God equips those He calls. Step boldly into your potential and trust Him to lead you into a life that glorifies Him and transforms others. The question is simple: are you ready to commit to your greatness? The choice is yours—and it starts today.

So, take a moment to sit with the truth you've uncovered. Reflection is not just about looking back—it's about gathering the wisdom, courage, and clarity you need to move forward. And rising is not just about taking action—it's about stepping into the life you were created for, one bold decision at a time.

You are not the same person you were when you began this journey. You've grown, you've learned, and you've begun to see yourself and your life through a new lens. The challenges you've faced, the lessons you've learned, and the truths you've embraced have all prepared you for this moment. Now, it's time to rise.

Rising doesn't mean you'll never face obstacles or doubts again. It means you'll face them with a stronger sense of who you are and why you're here. It means you'll choose courage over fear, purpose over comfort, and authenticity over approval. It means you'll live a life that reflects the greatness within you.

So, as you turn the page to the next chapter, carry this truth with you: your past does not define you, your present does not limit you, and your future is waiting for you to claim it. You were created for more than survival—you were created for a life of meaning, impact, and joy.

The journey ahead is yours to write. Reflect on where you've been, rise to who you are, and embrace the life you were created for. The world is waiting for the gift that only you can bring.

You've stood at the mirror long enough.
That reflection of fear? Shatter it.
The image of your future? Wear it.
Step forward—the world needs
what only your unedited soul can bring.
—Tessy Tanyi

CHAPTER 7

WINGS OF CHANGE

*No More Boxes.
Only Wings.*

*You didn't choose the box—they handed it to you.
You didn't draw the lines—they told you not to cross them.
And somewhere along the way, you started to believe them.*
—Tessy Tanyi

The box was subtle at first.

A comment. A label. A quiet limitation wrapped in someone else's opinion.

"You're too much."

"You're not enough."

"People like you don't do things like that."

They tried to define you. Contain you. Reduce you to what they could understand. These voices—sometimes loud, sometimes whispered—begin to shape how we see ourselves. Over time, the box shrinks our vision, stifles our potential, and buries the boldness God placed in us from the very beginning. But here's the truth: you were never made for boxes—you were made for wings. Boxes keep you small. Wings teach you to soar. Boxes are built by fear, tradition, and assumptions. Wings are given by grace, truth, and courage. The box was never yours. You weren't created to live confined by fear, limited by others' expectations, or trapped by beliefs that don't align with God's Word. You were made for freedom. For transformation. For change. *And change has a rhythm—a divine timing.* It's like scripture tells us, "There is a time for everything, and a season for every activity under the heavens: a time to be born and a time to die . . . a time to embrace and a time to refrain from embracing" (Ecclesiastes 3: 1-2, 5).

In this chapter, we break the boxes—the labels, the limiting beliefs, the false identities—and begin to rise. Not just for the sake of change but for the sake of becoming who God has called you to be. Because once you realize the box was never yours, you're free to discover what was—your wings.

I believe this is your divine timing because breaking free is just the beginning. Stepping into who you're becoming means learning to walk in rhythm with the seasons God has appointed for your growth.

The timeless words in the above scripture we just read remind us that life is a series of seasons, each with its own purpose and rhythm. And now, dear reader, you stand at the threshold of a new season—a season of transformation.

The chrysalis cracks, the shell breaks, and the old is passing away. You've spent time recognizing the "eagle" within, shedding limiting beliefs, and catching glimpses of the magnificent creature you were always meant to be. But seeing your potential and becoming it are two very different things. This chapter is about stepping into that newness—taking ownership of the person you were designed to be, not the one shaped by fear, doubt, or external expectations.

This isn't just a suggestion; it's an invitation to live the most authentic and vibrant life imaginable. Enough theory. Enough dreaming. In the previous chapters, we laid the groundwork for transformation; now, it's time to build. This chapter is about practical application—the tangible steps you can take today to begin living as the eagle you truly are.

Transformation is not a passive process; it demands courage, commitment, and the willingness to step outside your comfort zone. It requires you to spread your wings, even when the winds of change feel uncertain. But remember, the eagle does not wait for the storm to pass—it uses the storm to rise higher. So, get ready to roll up your sleeves and start actively constructing the life you've been envisioning. The time has come to embrace your transformed identity, to step into the fullness of who you are, and to soar with purpose and confidence. Let's begin.

The whispers of the Divine have grown louder, and the call to your true identity is undeniable. But hearing the call is just the beginning. "Embrace the new you" is about answering that call. It's about surrendering to the process of transformation, allowing the Spirit to mold you into the image of the eagle God sees in you. This chapter is an exploration of faith, trust, and the beautiful journey of becoming who you were always destined to be. Prepare to be transformed from the inside out. The promise of a new you is exhilarating, yet the reality can be daunting. Old habits cling, familiar fears resurface, and the comfort of the familiar tries to pull you back. "Embrace the new you" isn't about pretending those challenges don't exist. It's about acknowledging them, understanding them, and equipping yourself to overcome them. This is where theory meets practice, where intention meets action, and where the journey of true transformation truly begins.

For most of my life, I lived in a box—a box built by others' expectations, my own fears, and the limiting beliefs I had unknowingly embraced. I was comfortable there because it was all I had ever known. The people around me knew me as someone who fit neatly into their narrative of who I should be. I didn't ruffle feathers, didn't step out of line, and certainly didn't dream too big. I thought that was just how life was supposed to be. But one day, everything changed. Through prayer, reflection, and meditation on the Word of God, I began to hear a voice deep within me—gentle but persistent. It was the Holy Spirit calling me out of my comfort zone and into something far greater. Through scriptures like 2 Corinthians 5:17— "If anyone is in Christ, the new creation has come: The old has gone, the new is here!"—I began to see myself differently. God didn't see me as someone trapped in a box; He saw me as an eagle, created to soar above the noise and live out His divine purpose for my life.

At first, this revelation was exhilarating. I felt free for the first time in years. I made up my mind to shed the limiting beliefs that had held me back for so long and allow the Holy Spirit to mold me into the person God had always intended me to be. But as soon as I started taking steps toward this new identity, the resistance came. People who had known me for years—friends, family members, even colleagues—started questioning me. "You've changed," they said, and not always in a kind way. Some accused me of thinking I was better than them because I no longer participated in certain conversations or activities that didn't align with my newfound identity in Christ. Others tried to remind me of my past mistakes as if to say, "Who do you think you are to try and be someone different?" Their words stung more than I cared to admit. They didn't quite know what to make of this new version of me. Some questioned my choices, while others outright resisted the changes they saw in me. They wanted me to fit back into their box, the one that no longer suited the person I was becoming. The tension became palpable as they tried to pull me back into old patterns and roles that felt safe for them but stifling for me.

The more I leaned into the new me, the more I felt the weight of rejection and misunderstanding. There were moments when fear crept in—fear of losing relationships, fear of being misunderstood, fear of stepping too far outside what felt familiar and comfortable.

I found myself at a crossroads. On the one hand, it would have been so easy to shrink back into my old self—to fit back into their box and avoid the discomfort of rejection or misunderstanding. After all, change is never easy. The unknown can feel terrifying when you've spent your whole life clinging to what's familiar, even if that familiarity isn't good for you.

On the other hand, there was this undeniable pull in my spirit—a call to rise higher, to embrace the eagle God saw when He looked at me. But stepping into that identity required faith and

> *The more I embraced this new identity, the less concerned I became about others' opinions or approval.*

courage that I wasn't sure I had. One night, as I wrestled with these conflicting emotions, I opened my Bible and stumbled upon Joshua 1:9: "Have I not commanded you? Be strong and courageous. Do not be afraid; do not be discouraged, for the Lord your God will be with you wherever you go." Those words hit me like a lightning bolt. God wasn't asking me to make this journey alone; He was promising to walk with me every step of the way—the Holy Spirit kept speaking gently but firmly, reminding me of the eagle within.

Through prayer and meditation on God's Word, He reassured me that He hadn't called me out of my comfort zone just to leave me there alone. His words of reassurance gave me strength when fear threatened to pull me back. I realized then that I had to pick a side. Either I could settle for a life of mediocrity and comfort—the life others expected of me—or I could embrace the new identity God was revealing to me through His Word. It wasn't an easy choice, but it was a necessary one. The next day, I decided: no more shrinking back. No more trying to fit into boxes that weren't meant for me. Instead, I chose to lean fully into who God was calling me to be. It wasn't without challenges—there were moments when fear crept back in and whispered lies about how much easier it would be to go back to my old ways. But every time those thoughts arose, I reminded myself of who God says I am: His masterpiece (Ephesians 2:10), fearfully and wonderfully made (Psalm 139:14), and an eagle designed to soar (Isaiah 40:31).

As time went on, something amazing happened. The more I embraced this new identity, the less concerned I became about others' opinions or approval. Some relationships naturally fell away as people realized they couldn't hold me back anymore—and that was okay. God brought new people into my life who encouraged and supported this transformation.

Looking back now, I can see how pivotal that season was in shaping who I am today. Change was hard—harder than anything I'd ever done before—but it was worth every tear shed and every fear confronted because on the other side of that struggle was freedom— freedom to live authentically as the person God created me to be. So, if you find yourself standing at a similar crossroads today, let me encourage you: don't settle for less than what God has planned for your life. Yes, change is uncomfortable; yes, it will stretch you in ways you never imagined. But remember this: eagles weren't created for cages—they were made to soar. And so were you!

OVERCOMING LIMITING BELIEFS

Here are some of the limiting beliefs I had to shed to follow God, step into ministry, write books, empower women, preach, teach, raise godly children, and be a submissive wife according to biblical standards:

1) **Follow God**

Limiting Belief #1: "I'm not good enough for God to use me."

Truth #1: God doesn't call the qualified; He qualifies the called. His strength is made perfect in my weakness (2 Corinthians 12:9).

Limiting Belief #2: "I have to be perfect before I can follow God fully."

Truth #2: God works through imperfect people. He refines us as we walk with Him (Philippians 1:6).

2) **Step into Ministry**

Limiting Belief #1: "I'm not bold enough to share the gospel or lead others."

Truth #1: Boldness comes from the Holy Spirit, not from my own strength (Acts 4:29-31).

Limiting Belief #2: "I'm too young or inexperienced to make an impact."

Truth #2: God uses people of all ages and backgrounds. Timothy was young but still called to lead (1 Timothy 4:12).

Limiting Belief #3: "I'll fail if I step out in ministry."

Truth #3: Success in ministry is measured by obedience, not outcomes. God equips those He calls (Hebrews 13:21).

3) **Write Books**

Limiting Belief #1: "I don't have anything valuable to say."

Truth #1: My story and experiences matter because they reflect God's work in my life (Revelation 12:11).

Limiting Belief #2: "I'm not a good enough writer to write a book."

Truth #2: God gives wisdom and creativity when we trust Him with our gifts (James 1:5).

Limiting Belief #3: "No one will read or care about what I write."

Truth #3: My responsibility is to obey God's calling; He will determine the impact (Isaiah 55:11).

4) **Empowering Women**

Limiting Belief #1: "As a woman, I should stay in the background and not lead."

Truth #1: Women throughout Scripture—like Deborah, Esther, and Priscilla—were used mightily by God to lead and empower others (Judges 4:4; Acts 18:26).

Limiting Belief #2: "Empowering women might seem prideful or self-serving."

Truth #2: Empowering others is an act of service that glorifies God when done with humility (Philippians 2:3-4).

5) **Preaching and Teaching**

Limiting Belief #1: "I'm not knowledgeable enough about Scripture to teach others."

Truth #1: The Holy Spirit teaches us and brings understanding as we study and share His Word (John 14:26).

Limiting Belief #2: "People won't take me seriously as a preacher or teacher."

Truth #2: My authority comes from God's Word, not from human approval (2 Timothy 3:16-17).

6) **Raising Godly Children**

Limiting Belief #1: "I'll never be able to raise children who follow Christ in today's world."

Truth #1: God equips parents with wisdom and grace for the task of raising children in His ways (Proverbs 22:6; James 1:5).

Limiting Belief #2: "I have to be a perfect parent for my children to turn out right."

Truth #2: My role is to model faithfulness and trust God with the results (Deuteronomy 6:6-7).

7) **Being a Submissive Wife According to Biblical Standards**

Limiting Belief #1: "Submission means losing my identity or voice in the marriage."

Truth #1: Biblical submission is about mutual respect and partnership under Christ's leadership—not silence or inferiority (Ephesians 5:21-33).

Limiting Belief #2: "If I submit, my needs won't be met."
<u>Truth #2:</u> Submission is an act of trust in both God and your spouse, knowing that Christ-centered love seeks the good of both partners (Colossians 3:18-19).

The key to overcoming these limiting beliefs was replacing them with empowering truths from Scripture. By meditating on God's Word daily, praying for boldness, and stepping out in faith despite fear, I began to shed these lies one by one. Trusting that God's power works through my weaknesses allowed me to embrace His calling in every area of my life.

In addition to the above beliefs, "I do not have anyone to help me if I step out to do what God is calling me to do," was particularly antagonizing. This is a common fear that can hold many people back from pursuing whatever God requests of them—whether it be going back to school and getting a degree, starting a business, starting a career or transitioning to a different one, taking in an orphan(s), or starting a ministry. However, it's important to recognize this as a limiting belief that doesn't align with the truth of God's Word and His character. Here's how we can challenge and reframe this belief:

God Promises His Presence: In Joshua 1:9, He says, "Have I not commanded you? Be strong and courageous. Do not be afraid; do not be discouraged, for the LORD your God will be with you wherever you go." You are never truly alone when you step out in faith.

The Holy Spirit Is Your Helper: Jesus promised us the Holy Spirit as our Helper and Guide. John 14:26 says, "But the Advocate, the Holy Spirit, whom the Father will send in my name, will teach you all things and will remind you of everything I have said to you." The Spirit is always with you, providing wisdom, comfort, and strength.

God Provides Community: Often, when we step out in faith, God brings people into our lives to support and encourage us. Proverbs 18:24 says, "One who has unreliable friends soon comes to ruin, but there is a friend who sticks closer than a brother." Trust that God can provide the right people at the right time.

You Have a Responsibility to Seek Support: While God provides, we also have a role in building our support network. Joining a church, seeking God to find the right mentor, or connecting with like-minded believers can provide the community you need. Hebrews 10:24-25 encourages us to "consider how we may spur one another on toward love and good deeds, not giving up meeting together."

God Is Sufficient: Even if human support seems lacking, remember that God's grace is sufficient. Paul learned this lesson when he said in 2 Corinthians 12:9, "But he said to me, 'My grace is sufficient for you, for my power is made perfect in weakness.'" Instead of saying "I do not have anyone to help me," try reframing it as: "God is with me, and He will provide the support I need as I step out in faith to follow His calling."

Remember, taking that first step often requires courage, but it's in that step of faith that we often see God's provision most clearly. Trust in His faithfulness and take heart in knowing that you are never truly alone on this journey.

Some additional lies I had to shed were:

"I'm not smart enough to speak up with my ideas."

"Wanting more is selfish."

"I'm not creative or intelligent enough to start a company."

"I don't deserve happiness."
"I'm a victim."
"I'm not good enough."

I also had to challenge the idea that because previous endeavors had ended negatively, I should not try again. I learned to replace these negative thoughts with alternative beliefs, such as "I'm a good business writer," and use affirmations to retrain my brain to think positively. I realized that these limiting beliefs were not necessarily true and that I had the power to change them. So do you!

Now, let me ask you, what are some of the limiting beliefs you're struggling with today? Take a moment to reflect on your own life. Are there areas where you feel stuck, held back, or unsure of your ability to move forward? Often, it's not our circumstances but our beliefs that keep us from stepping into the fullness of who God created us to be.

> *These beliefs are not from God. They are lies designed to keep you grounded when God has called you to soar.*

Do you believe you're not good enough to follow God's calling for your life?

Do you feel like your past mistakes disqualify you from being used by God?

Are you afraid of failing if you step out in faith?

Do you think you're too young, too old, or too inexperienced to make a difference?

Do you feel like your voice doesn't matter or that no one will listen to what you have to say?

Are you struggling with doubts about being a good parent, spouse, leader, or friend?

These are just a few examples of limiting beliefs that can creep into our minds and hold us back. Maybe yours sounds different. Maybe it's something like:

"I'm not creative enough to pursue my dreams."

"I'll never be able to overcome this struggle or addiction."

"I'm not smart enough, strong enough, or brave enough."

Whatever your limiting belief is, I want to challenge you today: shed it off! These beliefs are not from God. They are lies designed to keep you grounded when God has called you to soar. Here's how you can start breaking free:

1) **Identify the Lie:** What is the belief that's holding you back? Write it down and be honest with yourself about how it makes you feel and how it's affecting your life.

   Replace It with Truth: Find a promise in God's Word that speaks directly against that lie.

   For example, if your belief is:
   > "I'm not good enough," replace it with Philippians 4:13 (NKJV): "I can do all things through Christ who strengthens me."
   > "I'm too broken for God to use me," replace it with 2 Corinthians 12:9: "My grace is sufficient for you, for my power is made perfect in weakness."
   > "I'll fail if I try," replace it with Isaiah 41:10: "So do not fear, for I am with you; do not be dismayed, for I am your God."

2) **Take a Step of Faith:** Don't wait until you feel ready—step out in faith today. Whether it's starting that ministry, writing that book, speaking up in a meeting, or simply saying "yes" to what God is calling you to do, take one small step forward.
3) **Pray for Strength:** Ask the Holy Spirit to help renew your mind and give you the courage to move past fear and doubt (Romans 12:2). You don't have to do this alone—God is with you every step of the way.
4) **Surround Yourself with Encouragement:** Seek out people who will speak life into your journey and remind you of who God says you are.

Remember this: You are fearfully and wonderfully made (Psalm 139:14). You are God's masterpiece, created in Christ Jesus for good works (Ephesians 2:10). You are more than a conqueror through Him who loves you (Romans 8:37). The same power that raised Jesus from the dead lives in you (Romans 8:11)! So, today, I challenge you—what limiting belief will you shed? Write it down. Replace it with truth from God's Word, and take one bold step forward toward the life He has called you to live.

The Scriptures guarantee us that in life, change will always happen. When change occurs, fear tends to grip us, and we become anxious because we do not feel in control of life. The amazing news is that we do not need to be in control of our own lives—the One who created us is in charge of everything if only we allow Him to be. No doubt that change can be overwhelming; however, instead of rejecting the change, it is far better to trust God and allow the change to grow us and make us more like Jesus in our responses and attitudes towards the change. God has promised never to leave us nor forsake us, no matter the circumstance. If we keep seeking

God and love Him through the process, then we are promised that all things will work together for those who love Him and keep His commandments (Romans 8:28).

Change challenges us in many ways. It challenges our existing beliefs, interrupts our thought patterns, and leaves us wondering if we will be able to adjust our existing categories. As a matter of fact, it is one of the most threatening things many of us face in life, and yet we encounter it often. The universe itself is changing. The world we live in is changing with highly sophisticated technical discoveries that have radically altered our lifestyle. On a daily basis, reports from the news focus on new changes occurring in our world.

Change, they say, is a constant thing. We as a people change. Do not worry when people tell you that you have changed, especially if the change was for good and to fulfill your divine purpose. God did not design you to remain the same.

When people cannot fit you into their "box," they speak against you. That is not new. Jesus Christ was spoken against. People indeed change for different reasons. Some adjust to their moods and circumstances, while the environment shapes others. You may have come across an individual who is in a good mood today and an ugly one the next day. I have known several people like that—it can be very stressful when we don't know who a person will be from one minute to the next. We feel uneasy when we don't know what to expect from our husbands, wives, parents, adult siblings, friends, colleagues, or even our bosses. Unfortunately, nice people occasionally get irritable and touchy. But fortunately, grumpy people sometimes get nicer. The underlying fact is that we all change.

We usually find these changes intimidating and unpleasant and wish we could keep things under our control. We desire things to stay the way they have always been because we find more security and comfort in the old and familiar; thus, we struggle to accept change. I don't believe we can do anything about it—we can't hold onto anything unchanging in a world where everything is so insubstantial and transitory. When we are no longer comfortable with what used to be so satisfying, that is change. When our old shoes wear out and we get new ones to replace them, that is change. Unfortunately, many people walk through their journeys with a pair of old shoes that no longer fit.

THE HUNGRY SOUL AND SEEKING HEART EMBRACE CHANGE

Someone once said, "If you are not hungry for God, you are probably too full of yourself." I believe this is true. In my case, I was too preoccupied with earthly things—fashion, makeup, hair, and the need to please friends and other people, that I got totally lost in the crowd. But thanks to God for coming to my rescue and helping me regain my true identity—the eagle He has created me to be.

After some of the encounters with the Holy Spirit I described in chapter 2, an unquenchable and indescribable hunger flooded me. The zeal to know God consumed me. I did not just want to know *about* God; I wanted to know *Him*—His heart, His nature, His thoughts, and His ways. My focus became learning everything there was to know about Him. I wanted to know what makes Him happy, what grieves His heart and makes Him smile, and how to please Him and bring pleasure to Him. I wanted to know How to gladden His heart, make His day, and understand why the shared blood of His precious son Jesus was worth it. I wanted to know where He lives, how He looks, and how He sees, talks, and acts. It's all I hungered for.

A deep hunger to know God for myself—not through the philosophies and theologies of any man—immensely consumed me. For the first time in my life, I came face-to-face with what the apostle Paul said in Philippians 3:10 (AMP):

And this, so that I may know Him [experientially, becoming more thoroughly acquainted with Him, understanding the remarkable wonders of His Person more completely] and [in that same way experience] the power of His resurrection [which overflows and is active in believers], and [that I may share] the fellowship of His sufferings, by being continually conformed [inwardly into His likeness even] to His death [dying as He did].

The unquenchable hunger that engulfed my soul led me to seek God desperately beyond what I can describe here with words. I began to pray to God like David said, "O God, You are my God; with deepest longing I will seek You; my soul [my life, my very self] thirsts for You, my flesh longs *and* sighs for You, In a dry and weary land where there is no water" (Psalm 63:1, AMP). I embarked on a spiritual quest in the passionate pursuit of Christ; I was willing to do anything to see and experience God's glory firsthand. I became unsatisfied with the status quo or living below the full potential of the true knowledge of God. All that I desired and all that my soul constantly longed for was to dwell in His presence and worship Him, fellowship with Him, and talk to Him like a friend—the kind of fellowship that means seeking His heart and not just His hands.

When you seek God's hands, you only get the blessings, but when you seek to know His heart, you get both the gifts and the Giver of the gifts. All I began to do was sit at His feet and worship Him, honor Him, adore Him, exalt Him, and tell Him how much I wanted Him to reveal His heart to me. I realized that everything I need in life is found at the feet of Jesus, and I began to say to Him, "Lord, show me what no man, book, or education can reveal to me." I also prayed, "Let no part of me belong to anyone else—Lord, I want to be wholly yours."

> *God does not fill already full vessels. He only fills empty vessels.*

As I became totally sold out to Jesus, God showed up, and I've never looked back. He showed up when I began to seek Him as if my whole life depended on finding Him. The beautiful song by Tasha Cobbs became my favorite words to God every morning, day, and night:

> *"Lord, if I Find favor in Your sight, Lord please Hear my heart's cry. I'm desperately waiting to be where You are. I'll cross the hottest desert; I'll travel near or far for Your glory."*[13]

And then His voice broke through:

> *"Forget the former things; do not dwell on the past. See, I am doing a new thing! Now it springs up; do you not perceive it? I am making a way in the wilderness and streams in the wasteland."* —Isaiah 43:18-19

---

[13] Tasha Cobbs, vocalists, "For Your Glory" by Mia Santai Booker, 2013, track 4 on *Grace*, Motown Gospel.

God wasn't just calling me forward—He was demanding a death. "Daughter," He said, "My standard does not change: Come empty, and see My glory." That's when it hit me: to truly know Him, I had to die first. Not halfway. Not bargaining. Nail my flesh to the cross—every fear, every old identity—so the new me could rise found only in Christ.

If you are going to experience the authenticity of God, you have to understand the principles of the unchanging God. It is a dangerous thing not to know God and assume you know Him. To have an intimate and experiential knowledge of God, you have to first "un-know" everything else. You have to empty yourself completely. God does not fill already full vessels. He only fills empty vessels. You must first empty yourself of your past achievements, bitterness, anxieties, fear and man-made opinions. You must lay aside all preconceived ideas, man-made traditions, and religious ideologies concerning God. These things will weigh you down. You will be too full of yourself for Him to fill you.

Our dear apostle Paul, although very learned, counted everything he gained as loss so that he may gain Christ. He said:

But whatever former things were gains to me [as I thought then], these things [once regarded as advancements in merit] I have come to consider as loss [absolutely worthless] for the sake of Christ [and the purpose which He has given my life]. But more than that, I count everything as loss compared to the priceless privilege and supreme advantage of knowing Christ Jesus my Lord [and of growing more deeply and thoroughly acquainted with Him—a joy unequaled]. For His sake I have lost everything, and I consider it all garbage, so that I may gain Christ. —Philippians 3:7-8 (AMP)

The apostle Paul's "gains" were his credentials, credits and successes, man-made doctrines, and preconceived ideologies, etc. We must be careful not to consider past achievements so important that they get in the way of our relationship with Christ. We must lay everything at the altar and let our primary goal be to seek and know Christ for who He is. Paul was so desperate to know Christ that after he carefully considered everything he had accomplished in his life, he wrote it all off as "garbage" when compared with the greatness of knowing Christ. In becoming the kingdom eagle, you must value your relationship with Christ more than anything else. Your ultimate goal must be to know Christ; the presence of God is so overwhelming that one can never get enough of Him. In my case, the more I know Him, the more I want to know Him. I realized that one can know about God by reading His Word, but to see His glory requires you to come into His presence.

YOUR GREATEST MIRACLES AWAITS YOU IN THE PLACE OF SEEKING

Hebrews 11:6 says, "And without faith it is impossible to please God, because anyone who comes to him must believe that he exists and that he rewards those who earnestly seek him."

What God wants to give to you is not just a car, house, job, spouse, children, qualifications, degrees, positions, etc. What God wants to give you is total salvation. This salvation comes from the place of continuous and relentless seeking. God will not only prosper you, but He will also protect you and ensure no sorrow is added to your riches. King David, from his personal experience, testified to this truth in Psalm 91. It is important to note, however, that the wonderful promises of this psalm are dependent upon meeting the conditions stated in these first two verses: "He who dwells in the shelter of the Most High will remain secure *and* rest in the shadow of the Almighty [whose power no enemy can withstand] (AMP). Our desire should not just be to go to God in prayer with a shopping list of the blessings we want. Our desire should be to seek to know Him and dwell in His presence.

Do not allow yourself to be so preoccupied with getting that you cannot respond to God's giving. What man wants is blessing, but what God wants is fellowship. People who do not know God and the way He works fuss over what His hand can give them. As a kingdom eagle, you must strive to know both God and how He works. You must steep your life in God's realities and God's initiative so that you can begin to experience and enjoy God's provisions. As you begin to spend quality time alone with God, He will reveal Himself and His nature to you in a profound way, and you will depart from surface-level Christianity where most chicken believers reside. You will relate to the realities of His kingdom, and you will find that He will take care of all your needs and concerns.

As I transitioned from being a chicken Christian to becoming the kingdom's eagle, I remember vividly how daily fellowship with God became the most beautiful part of my day, and that has not changed and will never change. I sought God daily with all my heart, might, and soul, according to what He told me in Jeremiah 29:13 "Then [with a deep longing] you will seek Me *and* require Me [as a vital necessity] and [you will] find Me when you search for Me with all your heart" (AMP). As a mom and wife with a 9 to 5 job, I did not merely fit God into my schedule—I let my whole life revolve around God. My body always longed to be with Him; thus, I shut myself in alone with Him, worshiping Him and dwelling in His presence. All

I wanted was to dwell daily in His presence and carry Him wherever I went, whether at home, on the job, or on the road. Consequently, my mountain of problems became less important to me compared to my desire to stay in His presence, bowing before Him prostrate, breaking open my alabaster box, and letting heartfelt worship flow from me to Him with total abandonment of self.

In becoming the kingdom's eagle, you must be aware that God is not just a supermarket you visit with a shopping list of your problems. You must set aside time to pray and seek the Father's face, not just the blessings that come from His hands. As men long for God to bless them, God desires to fellowship with His people. All the blessings that men seek can be found at the feet of Jesus. As kingdom eagles, we must seek the Giver and not just the gifts. We must learn to enjoy His presence and spend time fellowshipping with Him and telling Him how much we love and desire Him more than any material increase.

If I had only one hour to pray, I would spend fifty-five minutes worshiping and praising God and the remaining five minutes presenting my requests before Him. When the Spirit led me to approach God this way, everything that was wrong in my life began to resolve before long. Every hopeless and shapeless situation started to take shape. My mountain of problems became plain as I saw the mighty hand of God resting upon each and every one of them. My life took a 180-degree turnaround from problems to miracles, lack to abundance, shame to fame, tears to laughter, ignorance to knowledge, fear to faith, weakness to strength, and grass to grace. I experienced deliverance and total healing in every aspect of my life: health, finances, marriage, and more. God is good!

ONE WITH GOD IS MAJORITY

When you allow God to transition you from a chicken Christian to the eagle Christian He created you to be, bear in mind that you will be exposed to change and transformation. You will go through a change process, and this is where many hold back and settle for the old, easy, and comfortable lifestyle that they are used to. You will also become vulnerable to the lies of the enemy. Satan will feed your mind so many lies, even through the voices of people you know. He will tell you that you cannot do it, and he will point out why you should remain as you are. Your friends, family, spouse, and other members of the body of Christ—especially those who have been there for you all along—will misjudge you, misinterpret you, misunderstand you, and malign you.

This is why you must make up your mind to rise up from the ordinary life of a chicken to the supernatural life of an eagle. You must not shrink back. You must not give ears to the naysayers. The only ones who can make it are those determined to leave surface Christianity and go deeper into Christ. Remember that you are the only one who is 100 percent responsible for your destiny. Whether you succeed in life or not is entirely up to you. How you handle the bricks thrown at you is up to you. What people want is for you to slow down and remain like them. But the truth is, you are not like them. Some folks may want you to see yourself as just another person. But they are 100 percent wrong. You must not look back. Change is constant. Do not worry when people say you have changed. You must embrace the change and move on!

Steve Maraboli famously said, "Life is a miracle. YOU are a unique expression of this purposeful miracle. Think of how GREAT that makes you. Live big! You are not here to dwell within the basement of your potentiality."¹⁴ You are different, unique, and fearfully and wonderfully crafted by God. You were designed to be extraordinary. If anyone tries to tell you who you are, look at them and tell them not to put a period at the end of their sentence because the pen of your destiny is not in man's hand; it is in God's hands, and He uses the foolish things of this world to confound the wise and the weakest things to confound the strong (1 Corinthians 1:27). Ayjee Grogan said, "Being different doesn't make you an outsider. It makes you unique and makes you stand out while looking into an unchanged world."¹⁵

Never forget that God is the writer of your destiny, not man. Men were not there when He wrote it, so they have no right to speak into what God has written. He sees the potential in you,

> *If you don't define yourself, the world will eagerly define you—and its definitions will always fall short.*

while men see the weaknesses. Only short-sighted people judge according to what they see with their physical eyes. The stone the builders reject is God's secret weapon. When men tell you that you are ordinary, refuse to listen to them, refuse to succumb, refuse to compromise, and refuse to blend in with them. You do not have to be normal. It is okay to be abnormal in the eyes of men. Do not

---

14 Steve Maraboli, Twitter post, February 12, 2014.
15 Ayjee Grogan, cited in Jeffrey A. Seddoh, "Dare to Be Different," *Medium,* 15 Oct. 2021, https://medium.com/@jaseddiee/dare-to-be-different-if-you-want-to-change-things-you-need-to-rattle-some-cages-shake-things-up-1a195227a2cd.

allow yourself to be seen through the eyes of men but through the eyes of God who loves you and gave Himself for you.

During my transition from a chicken Christian to an eagle Christian, I discovered the transformative power of speaking truth over myself. If you don't define yourself, the world will eagerly define you—and its definitions will always fall short. You must refuse to let others dictate your identity. Instead, stand before the mirror and declare with boldness: "I am beautiful. I am distinct. I am not like the rest. I am a special breed crafted by the hands of the Divine. I am spectacular. I am important. I am worthy. I am gifted and talented. I am the original, not a copy. I am one of a kind—there is no other version of me. I am irreplaceable.

These are not empty affirmations to stroke your ego; they are sacred confessions of who you truly are. God designed you with intentionality, weaving together a masterpiece that cannot be replicated. There is no one else on the face of this earth who carries your unique combination of gifts, experiences, and purpose. You are not an accident or an afterthought—you are a rare and irreplaceable creation, fashioned to reflect a facet of God's glory that only you can reveal.

And yes, you are indeed a rare species. God didn't make you to blend in; He made you to stand out. So, speak these truths over yourself daily. Let them sink into your spirit, reshaping how you see yourself and how you move through the world. You are not ordinary—you are extraordinary. Embrace it. Own it. Live it.

A warning: be careful of those who know your background; they can set you back to the ground, reminding you of a version of yourself that no longer exists. There comes a moment in every person's journey when the focus must shift from who walks away to who remains—God, the One who never abandons or forsakes His own. Even if the world around you is emptied, His presence is a constant, unshakable anchor in the storm.

Don't be afraid to sever ties with people or things that poison your spirit or dilute your purpose. Let go of what weighs you down, and make room for God to move in your life. Those who knew you "back then" will often try to dim the fire of your transformation—your newfound zeal, passion, and determination to rise as an eagle Christian. They may question your dreams, mock your goals, or dismiss your decision to stand out. But remember this: even Jesus, as He walked the shores of Galilee, faced rejection in His own hometown. A prophet is rarely honored among those who once saw him as ordinary.

One of the bravest decisions you'll ever make is to release the people who no longer align with your destiny. Not everyone is meant to journey with you into this new season. Some are tied to your past, and holding onto them will only hinder your flight. So, spread your wings, let go of what no longer serves you, and trust God to fill your life with those who will celebrate the eagle you've become.

The saying, "One person rightly positioned in your life is worth more than a crowd that is irrelevant to your purpose," is often attributed to Pastor Jairus Cephas. Everyone in your life is meant to be on your journey, but not all of them are meant to stay until the end. Letting go means realizing that some people are part of your history but not a part of your destiny. They are part of the journey but not part of the destination. One of the hardest things to do in life is to let go. Whether it is guilt, anger, love, loss, people, or betrayal, it hurts to let go, but most times, it hurts more to hold on. Change is never easy, but we do not rely on our own strength.

We rely on the power of the Holy Spirit that is at work within us to quicken us, help us, and give us the boldness to let go, forget what is behind us, and take hold of what lies ahead. Your past is not meant to define you, destroy you, deter you, or defeat you. Your past is only meant to strengthen you.

During your transition phase, you will experience what I call the great separation—a sacred moment when God gently pulls you from the crowd, setting you apart for His divine purpose. It's as if He lifts you from the noise of the marketplace and leads you into the quiet of His workshop, where He begins to shape you for what's ahead. This season, though necessary, can feel isolating. I remember it well—nights when the silence was deafening, and the absence of those I once called friends left me questioning everything. I cried out to God, "Everyone has left me. You're all I have now." Looking back, I chuckle at how I felt "stuck" with the Creator of the universe, as if His presence wasn't the greatest treasure of all.

In those moments of raw vulnerability, the Holy Spirit whispered truth to my heart, guiding me to this Scripture: "I'm off and running, and I'm not turning back" (Philippians 3:14, MSG). It was a reminder that the journey forward requires focus—eyes fixed on the goal, not the distractions behind me. The goal? To become the kingdom's eagle, soaring high above the storms, unshackled by the weight of past relationships or expectations.

This separation, though painful, is not a punishment—it's preparation. It's God's way of clearing the clutter, so you can hear His voice more clearly, see His path more vividly, and step into your destiny with unwavering confidence. So, when persecution comes and the road feels lonely, don't look back. Keep your gaze locked on the horizon, where God is beckoning you onward. Let this season mark the beginning of a new chapter in your life's journey—one where you rise unburdened and unstoppable. Trust me, in the end, it will all be worth it.

As you close this chapter, take a moment to celebrate how far you've come. The journey of transformation is not easy—it requires courage to shed old identities, faith to embrace the unknown, and resilience to rise above the noise. But here you are, standing taller, seeing clearer, and feeling the stirring of wings you may have forgotten you once had.

> *The journey ahead is not just about reaching new heights— it's about thriving in them.*

You've seen the box. You've felt the stretch of your wings. The chrysalis has cracked, the shell is breaking, and the old is fading away. This is the shift—because every transformation begins with awareness, but it finds its power in movement. Who you were or what others have said about you no longer defines you. The truth of who you are in Christ—a rare, irreplaceable creation, designed to soar—is what defines you now. The world may not always understand your transformation, but that's okay. You weren't made to fit in. You were made to fly.

As you prepare to turn the page, carry this truth with you: transformation is not a one-time event; it's a lifelong journey. Each day is an opportunity to spread your wings a little wider, to rise a little higher, and to live a little bolder. The sky is not your limit—it's your playground. But before you take flight, there is one crucial step you must take: preparation.

Even the mightiest eagle must ready itself before soaring into the unknown. In the next chapter, we will explore how to equip yourself for the journey ahead. From strengthening your spiritual wings to navigating the winds of change, this chapter will provide the tools and strategies you need to soar with confidence and purpose.

The journey ahead is not just about reaching new heights—it's about thriving in them. So, take a deep breath, steady your heart, and get ready. The flight of your life is about to begin.

> Transformation isn't a destination—it's your new oxygen.
> Breathe deep.
> Stretch those unfamiliar wings.
> The awkwardness you feel?
> That's just your soul remembering
> what your body never forgot:
> You were born airborne.
> —Tessy Tanyi

CHAPTER 8

PREPARING FOR THE FLIGHT AHEAD

Your Destiny Awaits

Imagine standing at the edge of a cliff, the wind whipping around you, your heart pounding with a mixture of excitement and trepidation. You've discovered your identity as God's eagle and embraced it, but now comes the crucial next step: preparing for flight. This chapter is your guide to strengthening your wings, building your courage, and readying yourself for the exhilarating journey ahead. Preparation is key to living as the kingdom's eagle. Just as a young eaglet doesn't immediately soar across vast distances, our spiritual journey requires intentional growth and development. This process isn't about achieving perfection—it's about consistent progress, trusting God's timing, and allowing Him to equip you for the heights He's calling you to reach.

In the pages that follow, we'll explore several critical aspects of your preparation:

Building Spiritual Resilience. We'll delve into practices that strengthen your faith, helping you weather life's storms with unwavering trust in God.

Shedding the Old Feathers: Learn how to let go of past hurts, limiting beliefs, and behaviors that no longer serve your new identity in Christ.

The Power of Waiting: Discover the transformative potential in seasons of waiting, and how to trust God's perfect timing for your life.

Learning to Confront Fear: We'll tackle common fears head-on, equipping you with biblical strategies to overcome anxiety and doubt.

Embracing Your Eagle Identity: Explore what it truly means to accept and live out the truth that God calls you an eagle.

Each section of this chapter is designed to strengthen a different aspect of your spiritual preparedness. Like an eagle testing its wings before that first flight, you'll find practical exercises, biblical insights, and personal stories that will help you build confidence in your God-given abilities.

Remember, this journey of preparation isn't about striving in your own strength. It's about allowing God to equip and empower you for the incredible adventure He has planned. Every moment spent in preparation is bringing you closer to the life of freedom, purpose, and abundance He has designed for you. As we embark on this crucial phase of your journey, open your heart to God's transformative work. Trust in His process, knowing that He is faithful to complete the good work He has begun in you (Philippians 1:6). Are you ready to spread your wings and prepare for the flight of a lifetime? Let's begin!

BUILDING SPIRITUAL RESILIENCE

Have you ever watched an eagle in the early stages of learning to fly? It doesn't soar effortlessly right away. Instead, it spends time building strength, practicing its movements, and learning to trust the wind beneath its wings. Similarly, our spiritual journey requires intentional effort to grow stronger and more resilient. In today's fast-paced world, where instant gratification is the norm, the process of spiritual growth can seem frustratingly slow. We often expect immediate results in our faith journey, much like we expect instant downloads or same-day deliveries. However, true spiritual resilience is built over time, through consistent practice and unwavering trust in God's process.

I remember a young woman named Sarah who came to our church's youth group feeling lost and overwhelmed. She had grown up in a Christian home but struggled to make her faith her own in college. The pressures of academic life, social expectations, and the constant bombardment of conflicting worldviews had left her feeling spiritually weak and uncertain. Sarah's journey reminds me of Isaiah 40:31, which says, "But those who hope in the LORD will renew their strength. They will soar on wings like eagles; they will run and not grow weary, they will walk and not be faint." This promise isn't about instant transformation but about the renewal that comes from consistently placing our hope in the Lord.

Over the course of a year, we watched Sarah slowly build her spiritual muscles. She started small—committing to a daily devotional app on her phone, joining a weekly Bible study, and volunteering at a local shelter once a month. It wasn't always easy. There were days when she felt like she was making no progress at all. But gradually, we saw her faith deepen and her resilience grow.

In my own life, I've experienced seasons of spiritual drought where I felt drained and unsure if I could keep going. I remember a particularly challenging time in 2024 when my business faced a major setback, and simultaneously, a close family member was diagnosed with a serious illness. The weight of these trials left me feeling spiritually exhausted and questioning God's plan. It was during this time that I learned the crucial importance of relying on God's strength rather than my own. I had to intentionally carve out time for prayer, even when I felt too busy or too tired. Two times a week, I joined an early morning prayer group that met at 5 a.m., set my alarm for a personal Bible study three times a week, and asked a friend to constantly check in with me for accountability. At first, it felt like additional obligations in an already overwhelming schedule. But over time, it became a lifeline. Through these practices and the encouragement of others, I began to see my resilience grow. It wasn't about being strong on my own—it was about trusting in His power to sustain me. I learned that spiritual resilience isn't the absence of struggle but the ability to face challenges with faith and perseverance.

In today's digital age, building spiritual resilience might look different than it did for previous generations. It might involve using faith-based apps for daily reminders and devotionals, participating in online prayer groups, or listening to spiritual podcasts during your commute. The key is consistency and intentionality in whatever practices you choose.

As we prepare for the flight ahead in our spiritual journey, let's remember that, like the young eagle, we're not expected to soar effortlessly from day one. Our growth comes through daily choices to trust God, engage with His Word, and lean on the support of our faith community. It's a process that requires patience, perseverance, and a willingness to keep trying even when we don't see immediate results.

In a world that often feels chaotic and unpredictable, developing spiritual resilience is more important than ever. It's what allows us to face life's challenges with grace, to maintain hope in difficult times, and to be a source of strength for others. As we continue to hope in the Lord and renew our strength, we'll find ourselves increasingly able to soar above life's storms, run without growing weary, and walk without fainting (Isaiah 40:31).

SHEDDING THE OLD FEATHERS

"I let go of regret and create space for new beginnings."[16]

—Phoebe Garnsworthy

An eagle goes through a remarkable process called molting, where it sheds old feathers to make way for new growth. This isn't just a biological necessity—it's a powerful metaphor for our spiritual lives. To fully step into the future God has for us, we must be willing to let go of the past: old wounds, failures, regrets, and even outdated ways of thinking. Holding on to what no longer serves us can weigh us down, preventing us from soaring to the heights God has planned. In 2 Corinthians 5:17, we're reminded of this truth: "Therefore, if anyone is in Christ, the new creation has come: The old has gone, the new is here!" Letting go of the past doesn't mean ignoring it or pretending it didn't happen; it means releasing its hold on you

---

16 Pheobe Garnsworthy, "I let go of regret and create space for new beginnings," Phoebe Garnsworthy.com, https://www.phoebegarnsworthy.com/spiritual-practices-for-letting-go-moving-forward/.

and allowing God to transform you into something new. It's about creating space for growth, healing, and renewal.

Holding onto what weighs us down is a setup for delays and limitations and can hinder us from moving forward. I remember a season in my life when I was carrying the weight of guilt from past mistakes. I had made poor decisions in relationships and career choices that left me feeling disqualified from God's purpose. I replayed those failures over and over in my mind, as if punishing myself would somehow make up for them. But all it did was keep me stuck. I felt like I was trying to run a race while dragging a heavy anchor behind me. One day, during my quiet time with God, I came across Isaiah 43:18-19: "Forget the former things; do not dwell on the past. See, I am doing a new thing! Now it springs up; do you not perceive it?" It was as if God was speaking directly to my heart. He wasn't asking me to ignore my past but to stop letting it define me. He was inviting me to trust Him with my brokenness and believe that He could create something beautiful out of it.

Letting go wasn't easy. It required courage and intentionality. I had to confront painful memories and forgive myself for mistakes I had made. I also had to let go of resentment toward others who had hurt me. One of the hardest parts was surrendering my need for control—releasing my grip on how I thought my life should have turned out. I'll never forget one particular moment when this lesson hit home. A close friend betrayed my trust in a way that left me deeply hurt and angry. For months, I held onto that bitterness, replaying the situation in my mind and wishing things had been different. But then I realized something: my refusal to let go wasn't hurting them—it was hurting me. It was holding me back from experiencing the peace and freedom God wanted for me. Through prayer and journaling, I began to release that hurt into God's hands. It didn't happen overnight, but little by little, I felt the weight lift off my shoulders. In its place came a sense of peace and clarity that allowed me to move forward.

In today's world, many people struggle with regret—whether it's over missed opportunities, broken relationships, or unfulfilled dreams. We live in an age where social media constantly reminds us of what others seem to have achieved while we feel stuck in our own shortcomings. But regret is like an old feather that needs to be shed—it serves no purpose other than keeping us grounded. A practical exercise that helped me release regret was journaling about lessons learned from past mistakes. Instead of focusing on what went wrong, I began writing down how those experiences shaped me into who I am today. For example:

> *It's not about erasing our history but about allowing God to redeem it.*

» A failed business venture taught me resilience and creativity.
» A broken relationship deepened my understanding of forgiveness.
» A missed opportunity reminded me to trust God's timing rather than my own.

Each regret became an opportunity for growth rather than a source of shame.

Letting go creates space for something better—something new—to take root in our lives. Just as an eagle's new feathers allow it to soar higher than before, releasing the past enables us to step into greater freedom and purpose. It's not about erasing our history but about allowing God to redeem it. In today's fast-paced world, we're often encouraged to "move on" without truly processing our pain. Truly letting go might look like:

» Taking time for reflection through journaling or prayer.
» Seeking counseling or mentorship to address unresolved issues.
» Where necessary, addressing conflict through healthy communication rather than bottling up hurts and disappointments.
» Practicing daily affirmations like: "I let go of regret and create space for new beginnings."

What are you holding onto today that's weighing you down? Is it guilt over a mistake? Anger toward someone who hurt you? Fear of stepping into the unknown? Take a moment to identify those "old feathers" and ask yourself: what is this costing me? Then, bring those burdens before God in prayer. Trust Him with your pain, your regrets, and your fears. Remember His promise in Matthew 11:28, 30: "Come to me, all you who are weary and burdened, and I will give you rest. . . . For my yoke is easy and my burden is light." Shedding old feathers isn't easy—it takes courage and faith—but it's necessary if we want to soar as kingdom eagles. When we let go of what no longer serves us, we create space for God's transformative work in our lives. And as we embrace His renewal, we'll find ourselves rising higher than we ever thought possible. So, today, take that first step toward freedom. Release what's holding you back and trust that God is doing a new thing in your life—you were made to soar!

THE POWER OF WAITING

Eagles don't just take off at any random moment; they wait patiently for the right wind currents to lift them effortlessly into the sky. This isn't laziness or hesitation—it's wisdom. They know that flying against the wind in their own strength would exhaust them, but they can soar with ease when they wait for the right moment. In the same way, waiting is an essential part of our spiritual journey. Trusting God's timing can be one of the most challenging aspects of faith, but it's also one of the most rewarding. Ecclesiastes 3:11 reminds us, "He has made everything beautiful in its time." This verse is a powerful reminder that God's timing is perfect, even when it doesn't align with our own plans or expectations. Waiting on Him is an act of trust and surrender, an acknowledgment that His plans for us are good and that He sees the bigger picture we often cannot.

I'll be honest—there have been seasons in my life when waiting felt unbearable. I remember a time when I was praying for clarity about a career decision. I had been working in a job that felt unfulfilling, and I was desperate for change. I prayed fervently for direction, expecting God to respond immediately with a clear answer. But instead, there was silence. Days turned into weeks, and weeks turned into months. I began to question if God was even listening. During that season, I wrestled with impatience and frustration. I wanted answers now—not later. But as I spent time in prayer and meditated on scriptures like Isaiah 40:31, "But those who wait on the Lord shall renew their strength; they shall mount up with wings like eagles," I began to realize that waiting wasn't wasted time. It was preparation time.

Looking back, I can see how God used that season of waiting to refine me. He taught me patience and trust, but, more importantly, He prepared me for what was ahead. If He had given me what I wanted immediately, I wouldn't have been ready to handle it. The delay wasn't denial—it was grace. For example, during that waiting period, I started volunteering at a local non-profit organization. At first, it seemed unrelated to my career goals, but it ended up being a pivotal experience that shaped my calling. The skills I learned there and the connections I made eventually opened doors to opportunities far greater than anything I could have planned on my own. I've also seen this truth play out in relationships. There was a time when I was praying for a breakthrough in a strained friendship. I wanted reconciliation to happen instantly, but it took years of prayer and small steps of obedience before healing finally came. In hindsight, I can see how God used that time to work on both of our hearts individually before bringing us back together.

> *Waiting doesn't mean doing nothing—it means actively trusting God while preparing your heart for what's ahead.*

One of the most profound lessons I've learned is that God's timing often doesn't make sense at the moment—but it always makes sense in hindsight. When we're in the middle of waiting, it can feel like nothing is happening. But behind the scenes, God is aligning circumstances, preparing hearts, and orchestrating details we can't yet see. Think about Joseph in the Bible. After his brothers sold him into slavery and he spent years in prison for a crime he didn't commit, Joseph must have wondered why God was delaying his deliverance. But when the time was right, God elevated him to a position of power in Egypt—not just for Joseph's benefit but to save an entire nation (Genesis 50:20). Joseph's story reminds us that waiting is never wasted when we trust God's plan.

Waiting doesn't mean doing nothing—it means actively trusting God while preparing your heart for what's ahead. Here are some practical steps you can take during seasons of waiting:

1) **Seek God Daily:** Spend time in prayer and His Word to strengthen your faith and stay connected to His voice.
2) **Focus on Growth:** Use this time to develop skills or work on areas where God may be refining you.
3) **Serve Others:** Look for ways to bless others while you wait—it shifts your focus from frustration to purpose.
4) **Trust His Promises:** Write down scriptures about God's faithfulness and meditate on them when doubt creeps in.
5) **Surrender Control:** Release your timeline to Him and trust that His plans are better than yours (Jeremiah 29:11).

LEARNING TO CONFRONT FEAR

Fear is one of the most common and paralyzing emotions we face as humans. It whispers lies that keep us from stepping into our God-given purpose, convincing us that we are not strong enough, brave enough, or capable enough to overcome the challenges ahead. But as believers, we are called to confront fear head-on, drawing strength from God and learning from the boldness of the eagle—a creature that embodies courage and resilience. The Bible often associates strength, courage, and victory with the eagle. As believers, we are expected to soar spiritually and in all areas of life with the strength of an eagle. The Greek word for strength, *dunamis,* speaks not only of physical power but also of moral fortitude and courage.

This kind of strength enables us to rise above fear, face challenges boldly, and live victoriously in Christ.

Eagles are remarkable creatures known for their boldness and fearlessness. Neither storms nor predators intimidate them. When faced with a poisonous snake, an eagle doesn't retreat in fear—it attacks with precision, tearing off the snake's head with its powerful beak. When storms arise, eagles don't cower or hide; instead, they soar directly into the storm, using its winds to propel them higher. This fearless nature is a powerful lesson for every one of us. Fear will always try to stop us from fulfilling God's purpose for our lives. It may come in the form of doubt, anxiety, or intimidation. But like the eagle, we are called to confront fear with courage and trust in God's strength to carry us through.

The story of the Israelites at the Red Sea is a perfect example of confronting fear with faith. Trapped between Pharaoh's army behind them and the Red Sea in front of them, their situation seemed hopeless. Fear gripped their hearts as they cried out to Moses for help. But Moses responded with these powerful words: "Do not be afraid. Stand firm and you will see the deliverance the LORD will bring you today. . . . The LORD will fight for you; you need only to be still" (Exodus 14:13-14). In that moment of fear, God showed His power by parting the Red Sea, making a way where there had been none. The Israelites walked through on dry ground while their enemies were destroyed behind them. This miraculous deliverance reminds us that God is always present in our moments of fear, ready to fight for us and make a way forward.

In Deuteronomy 32:11-12, God compares His care for Israel to that of an eagle caring for its young: "Like an eagle that stirs up its nest and hovers over its young, that spreads its wings to catch them and carries them aloft." Eagles teach their young to fly by pushing them out of the nest—a terrifying experience for a fledgling bird. But as they fall through the air, their mother swoops beneath them with her wings outstretched to catch them if they falter. Similarly, God allows us to face situations that stretch our faith and confront our fears—not to harm us but to strengthen us. And just like the mother eagle, He is always there to catch us when we fall.

Fear comes in many forms in our modern lives: fear of failure, rejection, uncertainty about the future, or even fear of stepping into what God has called us to do. I remember the very first time when I felt God calling me to step out into ministry—to speak publicly about my faith and share His Word with others. The thought terrified me. What if I failed? What if people judged me? What if I wasn't good enough? For weeks, I wrestled with these fears until I came across Isaiah 41:10: "So do not fear, for I am with you; do not be dismayed, for I am your God. I will strengthen you and help you; I will uphold you with my righteous right hand." That verse became my anchor. I realized that confronting fear wasn't about pretending it didn't exist—it was about trusting God's promise to be with me in every step of obedience. When I finally said "yes" to His call despite my fears, I experienced His strength, carrying me through in ways I had never imagined.

> *Eagles don't let storms stop them—they use them as opportunities to rise higher.*

Here, I will share some practical steps that helped me confront fear. First, I had to recognize fear as a tool that hinders me from fulfilling my purpose. Second, I began to study the Bible, meditate on God's word, and renew my mind to align with God's will to combat fear. Third, I chose to trust in God's presence, sovereignty, and love for me. As I practiced these, my focus began to shift toward God, and the more I practiced, the clearer it became that fear is not from Him. Face fear with courage and kindness, understanding it deeply rather than trying to overpower it. The following additional tips will help you confront fear:

1) **Acknowledge Your Fear:** Don't ignore or suppress your fears—bring them before God in prayer and ask Him for courage.
2) **Meditate on God's Word:** Fill your mind with scriptures that remind you of God's promises and His faithfulness. For example, "For God has not given us a spirit of fear but of power and love and self-discipline" (2 Timothy 1:7, NLT) and "When I am afraid, I put my trust in you" (Psalm 56:3).
3) **Take Small Steps of Faith:** Start by confronting smaller fears as you build your confidence in God's ability to sustain you.
4) **Surround Yourself with Support:** Seek encouragement from fellow believers who can pray with you and remind you of God's truth.
5) **Focus on God's Power:** Shift your focus from your limitations to God's limitless power working through you.

Eagles don't let storms stop them—they use them as opportunities to rise higher. As believers called to live like eagles, we must learn to confront fear with boldness and faith in God's promises. Fear may try to hold us back, but when we trust in His strength rather than our own, we can soar above every obstacle. Remember this truth:

you were not created to live grounded by fear—you were made to soar! When fear comes knocking at your door, respond like Moses did at the Red Sea: stand firm in faith and watch how God delivers you. So, today, ask yourself: What fears are holding me back from living fully as the kingdom's eagle? Bring those fears before God and trust Him to give you the courage to rise above them. With Him by your side, there is no storm too great or challenge too daunting—you were made to fly!

As we wrap up this chapter, remember that you are the captain of your own ship—the pilot of your own flight. The direction you choose to sail and the heights you choose to soar are entirely in your hands. Don't wait for circumstances or others to dictate your path. Take control, set your course, and navigate with intention. You've strengthened your wings, tested the winds, and positioned yourself for takeoff. Now, it's time to leap into the unknown with faith and determination.

Preparation is not about having all the answers—it's about building the resilience, faith, and courage to face whatever comes your way. Trust that the God who called you to this journey has already equipped you for it. The tools, strategies, and truths you've gathered in this chapter are not just for your benefit—they are for the purpose you are about to fulfill.

So, as you stand on the edge of this new beginning, know that you are not alone. The same God who prepared you is the One who will guide you. The winds may shift, the storms may come, but you are built to rise above them. The sky is waiting, and your time to soar is now.

But soaring is not just about reaching new heights—it's about flying with intention. In the next chapter, we will explore how to align your flight with the greater vision God has for your life. This is not just about moving forward; it's about moving forward with clarity, focus, and a deep sense of purpose.

You were not created to fly aimlessly. You were created to soar with direction, to fulfill a divine assignment that only you can accomplish. Your journey is yours to shape, so start today, and commit to living with purpose. As you prepare to turn the page, get ready to discover how to align your wings with God's vision for your life. The journey ahead is not just about elevation—it's about transformation.

> The forecast says turbulence ahead.
> Good.
> Eagles don't train in still air.
> Your wings were made for this exact pressure—
> not to survive the storm,
> but to ride it higher
> than you've ever flown.
> —Tessy Tanyi

CHAPTER 9

SOARING WITH PURPOSE

*Aligning with Your
Divine Vision*

> "*Where* there is *no vision, the people perish:* but
> he that keepeth the law, happy is he."
> —Proverbs 29:18 (KJV)

> "*If people can't see what God is doing, they stumble
> all over themselves; but when they attend to
> what he reveals, they are most blessed.*"
> —Proverbs 29:18 (MSG)

Having prepared for your flight in the previous chapter, you now stand at the edge of your nest, ready to spread your wings and soar. This pivotal moment marks the beginning of your journey as an eagle Christian, fully embracing the potential God has placed within you. In this chapter, we'll explore what it means to truly soar with purpose, aligning every aspect of your life with the divine vision God has for you. Just as an eagle doesn't simply flap its wings aimlessly but rides the wind currents with intention and grace, you, too, are called to navigate life's challenges and opportunities with a clear sense of direction and purpose. We'll delve into:

- Understanding the difference between your mission and your vision
- Hearing God's voice
- Embracing your role as a contributor, not a consumer, and a person living on purpose, not just on pension
- Acting on your vision
- Living with passion and purpose

As Isaiah 40:31 reminds us, "But those who hope in the LORD will renew their strength. They will soar on wings like eagles; they will run and not grow weary, they will walk and not be faint." This chapter is your guide to living out this promise, helping you to not just fly but to soar with purpose and impact. Are you ready to embrace the heights God has prepared for you? It is essential to understand the power of vision in fulfilling your God-given purpose. Just as an eagle's extraordinary eyesight allows it to focus on its prey from miles away, clarity of vision is crucial for navigating your spiritual journey. Eagles are not distracted by obstacles or competing targets; they lock their gaze on their objective and pursue it with unwavering determination. You, as an eagle Christian, can develop and maintain a clear vision for your life and ministry. This involves more than just setting goals—it's about aligning your heart and mind with God's divine plan for you. As Dr. Myles Munroe once said, "Vision possesses you; you don't possess it."[17] When your

---

[17] Myles Munroe, cited in Olusegun Iyejare, "54 Inspiring Quotes on Vision by Dr. Myles Munroe," *Medium*, 20 Mar. 2024, https://medium.com/@mylesmunroeway/54-inspiring-quotes-on-vision-by-dr-myles-munroe-a0afba2bcd6f.

vision consumes you, it becomes the driving force that propels you forward, even in the face of challenges.

Psalm 90:12 reminds us, "Teach us to number our days, that we may gain a heart of wisdom." This chapter will challenge you to reflect on how you are using the time and resources God has given you. Are you living with purpose, or are you drifting aimlessly like a visionless Christian? Now is the time to focus your spiritual eyes on the path ahead, align yourself with God's divine vision, and soar into the extraordinary life He has prepared for you. Let's dive deeper into what it means to live as a visionary Christian who leaves a legacy for others to follow!

VISION VS. MISSION

A man with a mission needs a vision.

—Tessy Tanyi

Many people confuse their life's mission with their vision. After speaking with people from different walks of life, I have come to realize that many have confused their goals with their vision. I once asked a pastor what his vision was, and this is what he said: "To build a megachurch and have several thousands of people sit in my congregation each service." I told him that was not a vision; it was merely a goal. Your vision is the why behind the what. It's the underlying purpose that drives your actions and informs your goals. Your goals must align with your mission, and your vision should extend beyond material possessions or personal achievements. Instead, it should focus on something lasting, something that touches the lives of others and continues to impact the world long after you're gone. Luke 12:15 (NKJV) says, "One's life does not consist in the abundance of the things he possesses."

So, how do you discover your vision? You have to look within yourself. God has placed it inside of you. God has laid up hidden treasures for future supply (2 Corinthians 4:7). Your responsibility is to press inward and discover them. No one can do this for you. You can find it in the place of seeking. Seek the face of God in prayer, fasting, spending time in His Word, and cultivating a vibrant relationship with Him, and He will begin to reveal His purpose for your life to you. Vision is about God and not about us. No need to wonder why God said in Proverbs 19:21 that "many are the plans in a man's heart, but it is the Lord's purpose that prevails." We do not invent our own vision. God's purpose for our lives should be our vision. God tailors your vision because it uniquely belongs to you. As you continue to seek the face of God in prayer, it will become vivid to you.

I've asked countless people, "What are you going to do with your life? What is your vision?" Among all the responses I get, the most common ones are, "I want to get married, have a good family, build a big house, own multiple cars, and have a good career or own a good business," "I want to travel around the world," or "I want to have a hotel someday." These are not visions but mere goals. They are too general. Likewise, when I ask some Christians about their born-again experience and why they accepted Jesus Christ as their Lord and personal Savior, I get responses like these: "I want to go to heaven." "I don't want to go to hell." Choosing heaven over hell is good, but this shouldn't be the only reason for a child of God to come to his heavenly Father. The fastest way to heaven is death. If God wanted us in heaven immediately, He would have caused us to die immediately after confessing Him as our Lord and Savior. But He leaves us here on earth because He wants us to accomplish the purposes He has given us to fulfill.

We are saved not only to make it to heaven but to fulfill our earthly visions. Many people don't recognize the vision God has placed within them because they don't have a profound connection with Him. An integral relationship with God is the quickest and only way to know what vision He has placed within you. The only one who can unravel the hidden potential on the inside of you is the One who created you. Until you discover your vision and start fulfilling it, life is only a counterfeit.

For example, if you purchase a new television, you wouldn't know how to use it unless you understood the product's manufacturer. This is why we often refer to the manufacturer's manual. In the same way, we are supposed to look up to God and refer to His manual, the Bible, to learn about His unique products (you and me). Dr. Myles Munroe once said, "The greatest gift ever given to mankind is not the gift of sight, but the gift of vision. Sight is a function of the eyes; vision is a function of the heart. Eyes that look are common, but eyes that see are rare."[18]

It is interesting to note that the Bible doesn't say that a man's education makes room for Him but that his gift does. Some of you are barely living your lives out of what you learned in school and the job you managed to get. But you have never asked God, your Creator, what He created you for and the gifts He has placed within you to accomplish His purpose. Simply defined, vision is "a revelation of where you are going." Where there is no revelation of your

---

18 Myles Munroe, "Vision is the source . . . without vision," AZ Quotes, https://www.azquotes.com/quote/770789#google_vignette.

future, you lack personal discipline and self-control. But when you know where you are going, all your energy, time, and resources will go towards reaching that destination—those things that are in sync with your vision are the only things that will get your attention. Everything else becomes a distraction. You no longer consume everything because a clear vision automatically engenders focus.

Today, make a conscious decision to shift your focus from being a mere consumer to a purposeful contributor. Embrace the unique gifts and potential God has placed within you and begin to live a life that is aligned with His divine vision. The world is waiting for what only you can offer. I would like for you to pause and reflect on the following questions:

Movement without purpose is just motion, but with direction, it becomes progress.

» What are you contributing to the world around you?
» What specific gifts or talents do you possess?
» How can you use these gifts to make a positive impact?

HEARING GOD'S VOICE

Divine vision doesn't come from ambition—it comes from attention.

The clearer our vision, the more likely it is that we've been still enough, quiet enough, and surrendered enough to hear the whisper of God's voice. Vision is not just about seeing what's ahead—it's about hearing what Heaven is saying. When you're sensitive to God's voice, your sight sharpens. You don't just chase goals; you walk in direction. You don't just move fast; you move aligned. This is why alignment matters more than achievement. Because the only vision worth pursuing is the one God has authored.

In a world saturated with noise and distractions, the question, "Why are you here?" is more critical than ever. As the saying goes, "When purpose is unknown, abuse is inevitable." Without a clear sense of purpose, we risk drifting aimlessly, squandering our potential, and leaving a void in our hearts.

The first step toward living a fulfilling life is understanding your unique divine assignment. Just as Jesus knew His purpose—"I came down from heaven, not to do mine own will, but the will of him that sent me" (John 6:38, KJV)—we, too, must discover why God placed us on this earth. Many people, even Christians, struggle with this fundamental question. They go through life without a clear vision, simply reacting to circumstances rather than actively shaping their destinies. But the day you discover your "why" is the day you truly begin to live.

Your "why" is what provides you with a clear vision. Your vision is the driving force that propels you forward, guiding your decisions and shaping your priorities. It's the answer to the question, "Why am I here in this world?" And God Himself is the only One with that answer. He sent you here with a specific purpose in mind, and you will return to Him one day. What will you tell Him when that day comes? This question should guide your daily actions, helping you prioritize goals, eliminate distractions, and maximize your productivity.

You can examine how you spend your time and money to gauge the quality of your vision. Are these resources aligned with God's timetable for your life? A clear vision helps you discern between what is urgent and what is important, shifting your focus from mere activity to meaningful productivity. True fulfillment comes not from worldly success or material possessions but from living in alignment with your divine purpose. As I wrote in my book, *The End to Your Search,* only the One who created you can truly satisfy your heart. No friend, mentor, or spouse can fully reveal your purpose. It is a God-given vision uniquely tailored to you. You can attend countless seminars and conferences, but only God can ignite the spark of inspiration that will lead you to fulfill your destiny.

MORE THAN A CONSUMER LIVING ON PENSION

In today's hyperconnected world, it's easy to get caught in a cycle of consumption. We're bombarded with messages urging us to buy more, watch more, and experience more, often leaving us feeling empty and unfulfilled. But you were created for so much more than just consuming. You're not here to simply take up space or passively observe; you're here to make a unique contribution to the world. God doesn't create junk, and He doesn't sponsor flops. You didn't arrive on this earth empty-handed; you were born with treasures and hidden potentials waiting to be unleashed. The world is waiting for your manifestation, and my prayer is that they shall not wait in vain. As 2 Corinthians 4:7 reminds us, "We have these treasures in jars of clay to show that this all-surpassing power is from God and not from us."

Think of yourself as a container of God's contents, a custodian of His divine truths. You carry a great torch of destiny, and your responsibility is to align your will with His, turn that torch on, and let kings come to the brightness of your light. God loves you too much to see you as a failure. He created you in His image, which means you are inherently great. Your greatness is meant to be expressed. You are not here by accident; you are here on purpose. God knows the world needs something that no one else can offer but you. This means you are not just another copy; you are unique! God has deposited so much within you. Tap into your God-given potential and, through the direct access you now have as the Holy Spirit resides in you, begin to download the glory of God from the heavens to the earth. You are here to change the world with what is already inside of you—to be a history maker and to leave your footprints on the paths of your generation and generations to come. Don't be like those who only look forward to retirement with a house and a pension.

You can discover the reason you were born, and you can experience an exceptional life in light of that knowledge. You don't have to live an aimless, boring, ordinary, repetitive exercise because you were not designed to simply ride a rocking horse; you were meant to go somewhere—a divine destination.

As Dr. Myles Munroe aptly stated, "When you die, you're meant to leave this earth not on a pension but on a purpose."[19] Your dream is bigger than retirement. It's about leaving a legacy that reflects God's glory. I mentioned earlier that Proverbs 19:21 reminds us, "Many are the plans in a person's heart, but it is the LORD's purpose that prevails." No matter how busy or accomplished you may be, if you are not fulfilling God's purpose, you will remain unfulfilled. True success is not what you achieve but what God has called you to do. Jesus, a visionary man, declared, "For this reason I was born and for this reason I came into the world, to testify to the truth" (John 18:37, author paraphrase). What about you? Were you born

---

19 Dr. Myles Munroe, LinkedIn post, May 8, 2017, 9:05 a.m., https://x.com/rfactor1/status/861567651876941824.

to be a spectator or a catalyst? Are you content to accept whatever comes your way, or are you determined to make a difference?

Like Jesus, I believe I was born to share truth and empower others to live meaningful lives. I partner with God to transform, equip, and empower you to fulfill your divine destiny. It doesn't matter how much wealth or success you amass; if you neglect your spiritual destiny, you will fall short of your true potential. God sent Jeremiah to be a prophet, and He sent you with a divine assignment as well. What is it? Have you sought God's direction through prayer and fasting? Are you aware of the unique gifts and potential dormant within you? You can become God's voice—His ambassador—in this world. Unfortunately, many never consider these questions. They make shopping lists but fail to create a vision for their lives. But when we fail to fulfill our divine destiny, we fail both God and humanity. As I write, I am being God's mouthpiece, helping you understand kingdom principles. My earnest desire is that this book challenges you to unshackle your eagle wings so that you can soar.

God brought this book into your hands so that you might arise, mount up with wings as eagles, and fulfill His dreams for your life. It doesn't matter if you're eighteen or forty-five; if you don't know who you are, you haven't truly begun to live. You're merely existing outside of God's original design for you. Take this moment to reflect. What is your purpose? Why were you sent? It's time to trade the

> *God knows the world needs something that no one else can offer but you.*

chicken coop for the boundless skies and soar into the destiny God has prepared for you.

WHERE ARE YOUR "ACTS"?

In today's fast-paced world, information is abundant and easily accessible. With just a click, we can access countless resources on any topic imaginable. Yet, despite this wealth of knowledge, many people struggle to achieve their goals or fulfill their potential. The reason? We have become a generation of listeners and talkers rather than doers. The gap between knowing and acting has never been wider. This challenge is not limited to society at large—it has also crept into the body of Christ. Many believers consume sermons, attend conferences, and read Christian books yet fail to act on the truths they've learned. As James 1:22 reminds us, "Do not merely listen to the word, and so deceive yourselves. Do what it says." Without action, information becomes stagnant—a wasted resource that neither transforms lives nor advances God's kingdom.

In the church today, we see a troubling trend: believers moving from church to church in search of the "best" preacher or the most engaging message yet failing to apply the teachings they've already received. Pastors, too, can fall into the trap of prioritizing eloquence over truth, striving to attract audiences rather than inspire action.

> *Knowledge without action is like owning seeds but never planting them—it leads nowhere.*

This cycle of recycled information without application has diluted the power of the gospel message, reducing it to mere words rather than a demonstration of God's power (1 Corinthians 4:20). The result is a church filled with spiritual consumers rather than spiritual contributors—people who hear but do not act. This lack of action leads to purposelessness and unfulfilled potential. It's no wonder Jesus lamented through Jeremiah: "Hear this now, O foolish people, without understanding, who have eyes and see not, and who have ears and hear not" (Jeremiah 5:21, NKJV).

The difference between a visionary Christian and a visionless one lies in their response to God's call. Visionary Christians are driven by purpose; they seek God's direction through prayer (Philippians 4:6), align their actions with His will, and remain steadfast despite obstacles. They understand that having a vision isn't enough—it must be acted upon with faith and determination. On the other hand, visionless Christians live aimlessly, consumed by routine and distractions. They accumulate knowledge but fail to translate it into meaningful action. This wandering life is akin to carrying untapped potential—a tragedy that wastes the gifts God has entrusted to us.

The Acts of the Apostles were written because people acted on their faith. They didn't just hear Jesus's teachings; they lived them out boldly, transforming the world in the process. So, the question remains: Where are your "Acts"? What will be written about your life? If you find yourself stuck in a cycle of inaction or overwhelmed by information overload, it's time to refocus on what truly matters:

- » **Seeking clarity from God:** Spend time in prayer, and ask Him for a clear vision for your life (Habakkuk 2:2).
- » **Taking small steps:** Begin acting on what you already know instead of waiting for more information or ideal circumstances.
- » **Staying committed:** Let your vision consume you and drive your daily decisions, even when challenges arise.

Remember, knowledge without action is like owning seeds but never planting them—it leads nowhere. The world doesn't need more talkers; it needs doers who will step out in faith and bring God's vision to life.

As Psalm 90:12 urges us, "Teach us to number our days, that we may gain a heart of wisdom." Time is precious, and every moment wasted on inaction is an opportunity lost to glorify God and fulfill His purpose for our lives. The choice is yours: Will you be among those who act on God's Word and leave behind a legacy of faith and impact? Or will you remain among those who merely gather information without applying it? Let this be your moment to rise above mediocrity and embrace the life of purpose God has called you to live. Where are your "Acts"? It's time to write them with your life!

LIVING WITH PASSION AND PURPOSE

Imagine yourself as the captain of a ship, charting a course across a vast ocean. You are fully in charge of where you navigate to. Without a destination in mind, you're at the mercy of the winds and currents, drifting aimlessly wherever they may lead. But with a clear vision, you can navigate the turbulent storms, avoid distractions, and arrive safely at your desired destination. Your life is your boat, and if you do not know where you are headed, you will sail in any direction the wind takes you. But with a clear vision in mind, you will be able to avoid distractions and arrive at your destination. The profoundness of your vision determines whether you will compromise in the heart of the storm or die sailing through the storm. As the saying goes, "A man who does not stand for something will fall for anything." This holds true in all areas of life, especially when it comes to pursuing our purpose and fulfilling our potential.

Growing up, I witnessed firsthand the impact of living without a clear vision or sense of direction. One memory that stands out is seeing men at bus stops, hopping on and off different buses aimlessly—not because they had somewhere to go but simply to pass the time. Curious, I once asked an older person about their behavior, and the response was revealing—they had no specific destination in mind; they were just "whiling away" the hours. This experience wasn't just about passing time; it highlighted a deeper reality—without direction, movement can feel like progress, but it leads nowhere. However, I've also seen how having a clear vision, purpose, and opportunity can completely transform lives. The difference isn't in the ability to move, but in knowing where you're going.

This moment serves as a lasting reminder: movement without purpose is just motion, but with direction, it becomes progress. When people are guided by vision and equipped with the right tools, they don't just pass the time—they build, innovate, and shape a meaningful future. As someone once said: "Living aimlessly can be likened to dying bit by bit." If you're reading this book and feel like you're moving without a clear direction, it may be time to pause and reflect. Over time, I've come to understand that true poverty isn't just about a lack of money—it's about a lack of vision. Having a sense of purpose and direction can make all the difference in shaping a fulfilling and meaningful life.

As you close this chapter, remember this: soaring is not just about spreading your wings—it's about flying with intention. It's about aligning every beat of your wings with the divine vision God has placed within you. This is no small feat. It demands clarity to see the path ahead, courage to stay the course, and an unwavering commitment to the purpose you've been called to fulfill.

Soaring with purpose is not just about reaching new heights; it's about living with meaning. It's about understanding that every beat of your wings, every shift in direction, and every moment of flight is part of a greater plan. You are not just flying; you are fulfilling a destiny that only you can achieve.

As you continue to soar, remember this: your purpose is not a destination but a journey. It unfolds with every decision to trust God, every step of obedience, and every moment of alignment with His vision. The sky is vast, and your potential is limitless. Keep your eyes on the horizon, your heart fixed on His promises, and your wings steady in His grace.

Even the most skilled eagle cannot avoid the storms. Turbulence is inevitable, and adversity is part of the journey. In the next chapter, we will explore how to navigate the challenges that come with soaring to new heights. Storms may threaten to ground you, but they can also become the very winds that lift you higher.

You were not created to fear the storm; you were created to rise above it. So, as you prepare to turn the page, get ready to discover how to find strength in adversity, courage in chaos, and hope in the midst of the storm. The journey ahead may test you, but it will also transform you.

> Purpose isn't a destination—
> it's the wind beneath your wings.
> Stop searching for where you're going.
> Start becoming who you already are.
> The coordinates will follow.
> —Tessy Tanyi

CHAPTER 10

WEATHERING THE STORM

Finding Strength in Adversity

Life's journey is rarely a smooth flight. Just as eagles face turbulent winds and storms, we, too, encounter challenges that test our resolve, shake our faith, and push us to our limits. But here's the truth: storms are not meant to break you—they are meant to build you. They are the refining fires that reveal your strength, the fierce winds that teach you to soar higher than you ever thought possible.

In this chapter, we will explore how to navigate life's toughest moments with resilience and faith. Drawing inspiration from the eagle's ability to rise above the storm, we'll uncover how adversity can become a catalyst for growth, a tool for transformation, and even the very force that propels us toward our divine purpose.

Storms may try to pull you down, but they can also become the very force that propels you to greater heights. So, as we dive into this chapter, prepare to discover how to find strength in the struggle, courage in the chaos, and hope in the midst of the storm. The journey ahead may test you, but it will also transform you.

SOARING ON THE WINDS OF THE SPIRIT

One of the most awe-inspiring aspects of an eagle's flight is its ability to harness the power of the wind. Rather than exhausting itself with constant wing-flapping, the eagle waits for rising air currents to lift it effortlessly to great heights. This beautiful phenomenon mirrors our reliance on the Holy Spirit in our spiritual journey. Just as the eagle depends on the wind, we are called to rely on the Holy Spirit's guidance and empowerment. Zechariah 4:6 reminds us, "'Not by might nor by power, but by My Spirit,' says the LORD Almighty." This verse encapsulates a profound truth: our strength and success don't stem from our own efforts but from God's Spirit working in and through us.

I'll be the first to admit that I've often tried to navigate life's challenges in my own strength. There were times when I believed that sheer determination, careful planning, and relentless effort would be enough to overcome any obstacle. However, these attempts invariably left me feeling drained and overwhelmed. It wasn't until I learned to surrender to the Holy Spirit and invite His guidance and strength into every aspect of my life that I began to experience true peace and resilience in the face of adversity.

In my own journey of discovering God's purpose for my life, I've learned the importance of intentional prayer and listening. There was a time when I felt lost and unsure of my direction. I decided to dedicate specific time each day to pray and ask the Holy Spirit for guidance. At first, it felt awkward, and I wasn't sure if I was doing it right. But as I persisted, I began to notice subtle promptings throughout my day. Once, I felt a strong urge to call an old friend. It seemed random, but I acted on it. That call led to a profound conversation where I was able to offer encouragement during a difficult time in their life. Another instance was when I felt led to volunteer at a local food pantry. It wasn't something I'd normally do, but I followed the prompting. That experience opened my eyes to the needs of my community and ultimately shaped the direction of my journey. These small acts of obedience to the Spirit's guidance gradually revealed a clearer picture of my purpose. I realized that my unique gifts and experiences were meant to serve others in specific ways.

By consistently seeking God's voice and acting on His promptings, even when they seemed insignificant, I found myself aligning more closely with His vision for my life. This practice of spiritual awareness has become a cornerstone of my daily life, helping me navigate decisions both big and small with a sense of divine purpose.

EMBRACING CHALLENGES AS OPPORTUNITIES FOR GROWTH

As Jesus approached the culmination of His earthly ministry, He faced resistance from those who didn't understand His mission. This experience, described in Luke 9:51-53, serves as a powerful reminder that pursuing a God-given purpose often invites opposition. In today's world, this principle remains true. When you commit to following Christ and living out His calling, you may encounter resistance from unexpected sources, as Jesus warned: "If the world hates you, remember that it hated me first" (John 15:18). Consider the story of Igor Sikorsky, the aviation pioneer. Despite being told that human flight was impossible, he persevered to create the first successful helicopter. His determination in the face of skepticism mirrors the attitude we must adopt in our spiritual journey. Throughout history, those who've made significant impacts for God have faced strong opposition. This resistance often comes from spiritual forces that fear the potential of purpose-driven individuals. The very name "Satan" means adversary, highlighting the opposition we can expect when we step out in faith. However, this opposition should not discourage us. Instead, it can catalyze growth and deeper reliance on God. Like an eagle that uses adverse winds to soar higher, we can use challenges to strengthen our faith and resolve.

Pursuing your divine purpose, you will inevitably face opposition. This shouldn't surprise you. Satan may try to derail you using tactics like: fear, mockery and sarcasm, discouragement, exhaustion, threats and intimidation, negativity, others' anger, and more. Your response to these challenges is crucial. Giving in leads to quitting or settling for mediocrity. However, responding properly can

> *Opposition doesn't necessarily mean you're doing something wrong—it might mean you're doing something right.*

deepen your reliance on God and strengthen your resolve to fulfill your calling. For those pursuing a faith-driven purpose, remember that opposition doesn't necessarily mean you're doing something wrong—it might mean you're doing something right. Use it as motivation to press forward in your God-given purpose.

In today's fast-paced, interconnected world, pursuing your purpose often means facing significant opposition. Whether you're an entrepreneur launching a start-up, an activist fighting for social justice, or a person of faith living out your convictions, you'll likely encounter resistance. Like I said, this opposition can be a sign that you're on the right track. In our modern context, opposition might take various forms: skepticism from colleagues about your ethical standards, cancel culture and social media backlash for expressing your faith, family resistance to your commitment to service or ministry, online criticism and trolling, market competition and economic pressures, societal resistance to new ideas or beliefs, skepticism from colleagues about your ethical standards, family resistance to your commitment to service or ministry . . . the list can go on and on. The key is to view these challenges not as roadblocks but as opportunities for growth and refinement. Just as the Wright brothers defied skeptics to achieve human flight, today's innovators and change-makers must push beyond naysayers and obstacles. Just as successful entrepreneurs face setbacks before breakthrough innovations or social activists encounter resistance before creating meaningful change, your journey may require overcoming significant hurdles.

Consider how:
» Tech innovators face skepticism before revolutionizing industries
» Activists encounter pushback before achieving social reforms
» Athletes endure rigorous training before reaching peak performance

These challenges aren't meant to defeat you but to refine your skills, test your resolve, and prepare you for greater achievements. In today's digital age, even online criticism or social media backlash can be reframed as opportunities for growth and increased visibility.

Remember, cybersecurity experts know that hackers target valuable data. Similarly, if you're facing opposition, it may indicate that you possess something of value, be it innovative ideas, leadership potential, or the ability to inspire change. Thus, your challenges, whether personal, professional, or societal, can serve as a bridge to your next level of success. When you challenge the status quo or stand firm in your convictions, you're bound to face resistance. To navigate modern-day opposition:

- » Stay focused on your core mission and values.
- » Build a supportive community, both online and offline.
- » Use data and feedback to refine your approach.
- » Embrace adaptability and continuous learning.
- » Practice resilience and self-care.
- » Stay vigilant and aware of potential challenges.
- » Deepen your prayer life and dependence on God.
- » Surround yourself with supportive believers.
- » Keep your focus on Christ and His purposes.

Remember, true greatness often emerges from overcoming significant challenges. By reframing opposition as a sign of potential impact and an opportunity for growth, you can transform obstacles into stepping stones toward your goals. In this era of rapid change and global connectivity, your unique vision and purpose are needed more than ever. Don't let opposition deter you—instead, let it fuel your determination to make a lasting, positive impact on the world. Remember, meaningful spiritual growth and impact often come with a cost. It's when we move beyond comfortable religiosity to radical obedience that we truly begin to soar. As you pursue your divine calling, expect opposition, but don't let it deter you. By responding to opposition with faith and determination, you can turn challenges into opportunities for growth and greater impact in God's kingdom.

THE EAGLE CHRISTIAN'S PERSPECTIVE

Just as eagles thrive in storms, using powerful winds to soar higher, eagle Christians view life's challenges as opportunities for growth. In our fast-paced, often turbulent world, this mindset is crucial for personal and spiritual development.

Here are some key principles you must learn:

1) **Anticipate challenges:** Like eagles sensing an approaching storm, be prepared for life's difficulties.

2) **Use adversity to your advantage:** Instead of avoiding problems, face them head-on, using them to strengthen your faith and character.

3) **Rest in the storm:** Find moments of peace and reflection even in turbulent times.

4) **Trust in a higher power:** Rely on your faith to guide you through uncertainties.

In a world of constant change and disruption, view challenges as chances to innovate and adapt.

Use setbacks in your career or personal life as stepping stones to greater achievements. During times of social or political unrest, maintain a balanced perspective, focusing on personal growth and positive impact. Remember, true strength comes not from avoiding difficulties, but from learning to navigate them with grace and resilience. By adopting this eagle-like approach, you can transform obstacles into opportunities for personal and spiritual elevation.

Unlike other birds that hide from storms, eagles embrace them, using the wind to soar higher. Similarly, believers who walk in faith—eagle Christians—do not fear life's challenges but use them as opportunities for growth and strength. Instead of battling the storm itself, they recognize the true enemy behind it and face difficulties with boldness, prayer, and unwavering trust in God. Complacent chicken Christians, on the other hand, shrink back in adversity. They lack spiritual depth, relying on worldly distractions rather than God's Word. Instead of rising above challenges, they complain, blame circumstances, and give up easily. To succeed in life, we must have vision, remain focused, and trust in God's strength rather than our own. True promotion and purpose come from Him—not human effort. Just as the wise men followed Jesus's star, God alone orchestrates our destiny. Stop striving in your own strength—trust Him to elevate you at the right time.

> *When God places you, no one can displace you!*

Storms are not signs of failure or blockage—they are proof of progress. In the Bible, Joseph faced betrayal, slavery, and imprisonment, yet every challenge brought him closer to his destiny. No matter where he was placed, God's favor elevated him—from his father's house to Potiphar's estate, from the prison to Pharaoh's palace. Daniel experienced the same divine handover, rising to manage the Babylonian empire despite being in exile. You are not reading this by accident—God is setting you up for extraordinary relevance. What seems like a setback is actually a setup for your destiny. Every obstacle you face is pushing you closer to God's purpose for your life. Joseph's prison introduced him to the butler who connected him to Pharaoh, proving that even the lowest moments can be the doorway to greatness. Instead of complaining, embrace your challenges as refining fires. Just as the three Hebrew boys—Shadrach, Meshach, and Abednego—became known because of the fiery furnace, your trials are making you stronger, not breaking you. The battles you conquer will bring you into divine prominence. Stay strong, pray through, and trust God. As you do these, your mess will become your message, your pain will turn into purpose, and your test will shape your testimony. When God places you, no one can displace you! Those who once doubted you will witness God's glory upon your life.

EAGLE CHRISTIANS DO NOT COMPROMISE

In today's world of shifting values and social pressures, the concept of an "eagle Christian" remains powerfully relevant. These believers prioritize their relationship with God above all else, even when it means going against popular opinion or facing criticism.

Key characteristics of eagle Christians in today's context include:

1) **Integrity in a compromising world:** They maintain their values and faith, even when it's unpopular or could lead to social or professional consequences.

2) **Discernment in the age of information:** They filter the constant stream of voices and opinions through the lens of their faith, prioritizing God's guidance over societal trends.

3) **Courage in the face of cancel culture:** They're willing to stand for their beliefs, even when facing potential backlash or "cancellation" on social media or in their communities.

4) **Spiritual sensitivity in a distracted world:** They cultivate a deep connection with the Holy Spirit, learning to recognize and follow divine promptings amidst the noise of modern life.

5) **Authenticity in an image-driven society:** They prioritize genuine faith over appearances, refusing to compromise their beliefs for likes, followers, or social acceptance.
6) **Obedience over convenience:** In a world of instant gratification, they choose to follow God's leading, even when it's challenging or doesn't align with their immediate desires.

Eagle Christians understand that true fulfillment comes not from pleasing others or conforming to societal expectations, but from living out their God-given purpose with unwavering commitment.

> You cannot walk with God
> if you are not ready to let go of men.
> —Tessy Tanyi

Unlike chicken Christians, who complain and give up when faced with challenges, eagle Christians embrace difficulties as opportunities for growth. They understand that storms do not invalidate a vision; instead, they are part of the journey. True vision remains active even in chaos—circumstances or what the natural eyes can see do not dictate it. If your vision is only based on what is visible, it is merely a wish, not a true calling.

Many people abandon their dreams, saying, "I tried my best, but there was no way to achieve it." This mindset is limiting. Vision is not about doing your best; it's about making the impossible possible. When something doesn't exist, vision compels you to create it. Before a physical product or breakthrough materializes, it must first exist in the eyes of your heart—a vivid image of a preferred future that drives you forward.

Fulfilling your purpose is not a smooth, effortless journey. It requires relentless determination, perseverance, and the courage to push through obstacles. Many start with excitement, but when challenges arise, they lose focus and quit. Excitement alone won't sustain a vision—only unwavering commitment will. If your vision is real, you don't just start it—you live for it, and you pursue it with everything you have. The question is not whether challenges will come, but whether you are willing to keep going despite them. A life without purpose is a life unfulfilled. Excitement may get you started, but only determination will carry you to the finish line.

> *Storms are not meant to break us; they are meant to prepare us.*

THE PRICE OF TRUE PURPOSE

Every true vision must ultimately glorify God, not ourselves. We are created for His divine assignment, and our purpose is fulfilled in serving His will, not chasing personal glory. Many start their journey with enthusiasm, much like the disciples of Jesus, who eagerly followed Him, expecting power, position, and recognition. However, they failed to understand the cost of true greatness—the storms, the trials, and the sacrifices that come with fulfilling a divine calling.

The disciples (James and John) assumed that following Jesus meant an easy path to earthly authority, but they were unprepared for the suffering, rejection, and trials that came with His mission. When they asked to sit at His right and left hand in glory, Jesus challenged them, saying, "Can you drink the cup that I drink?" (Mark 10:38). They did not realize that this cup was filled with suffering, sacrifice, and ultimately, death. True vision is not about personal gain—it is about perseverance through adversity. Like James and John, many today rush into their calling with excitement, not fully grasping the challenges ahead. They are drawn by the dream but unprepared for the price. Vision is not just about starting strong; it is about enduring through the storms. The kitchen heat produces the dinner, and the fire refines the gold. Those who desire greatness must be willing to withstand the trials that shape them for it.

Are you truly ready for the vision you claim to have? Will you press on when faced with rejection, hardship, or suffering? Jesus knew His purpose and never wavered, no matter how fierce the storm. Like Him, we must fix our eyes on the ultimate goal and refuse to let adversity shake our commitment. Storms are not meant to break us; they are meant to prepare us. The question is—will you quit when the storm rages, or will you press forward until you fulfill your purpose?

As we conclude this chapter, I would like to remind you again that like eagles that soar above storms, using the wind to lift them higher rather than allowing it to bring them down, you are called to rise above life's challenges. Storms—trials, uncertainties, and obstacles—are inevitable, but as a kingdom eagle, they are unable to defeat you. Instead, you are meant to use them as stepping stones for growth, strength, and deeper faith.

Jesus reassured us in John 16:33, "In this world you will have trouble. But take heart! I have overcome the world." This doesn't mean life will be free of hardship, but it does mean that with God on your side, you can face every storm with courage. He has already secured victory, and in Him, you have the power to overcome.

I have faced my own share of storms—moments of loss, disappointment, and uncertainty. There were times when fear and doubt tried to take over, but in each storm, God reminded me of His presence. Instead of allowing difficulties to break me, I found strength in His promises. Looking back, I see how every challenge pushed me closer to my purpose and made me stronger in my faith.

Here are some practical tips to help you rise **above your storms:**

» **Pause and pray:** When facing challenges, take a moment to seek God's wisdom. Ask Him to help you see the situation through His eyes.

» **Anchor yourself in the Word:** Memorize John 16:33 and hold onto it as a source of strength whenever storms arise.

» **Shift your perspective:** Instead of asking, Why is this happening to me? ask, How is this shaping me? Trust that every storm has a purpose on your journey.

Carry this truth in your heart: storms do not come to destroy you—they come to elevate you. They are not your enemy; they are your training ground. Each gust of wind, each bolt of lightning, and each moment of turbulence is an opportunity to rise higher, to grow stronger, and to soar with greater purpose.

The storm doesn't define you, but how you rise above it does. Like the eagle, you were created to navigate the fiercest winds and emerge victorious. So, no matter how fierce the wind may blow, remember this: you are destined to overcome. Trust God, spread your wings, and soar. The storm is not your end—it's your beginning.

> Adversity isn't your opposition—
> it's your altitude adjustment.
> The same winds that snap kites
> are the ones eagles use
> to touch the sun.
> —Tessy Tanyi

CHAPTER 11

ASSOCIATIONS

A Pathway to Transformation or Deformation

Soaring above the storm is not a solo journey. The people you surround yourself with can either lift you higher or pull you down—they can be the wind beneath your wings or the weight that keeps you grounded. In this chapter, we will explore the profound impact relationships have on your destiny. Just as storms can elevate you, the company you keep can either propel you toward your purpose or hinder your progress.

Your associations are more than a reflection of where you are—they are a determinant of where you're going. The journey of life is not meant to be traveled alone, and the people you allow in your boat can either help you navigate the fiercest storms or capsize you in the process.

Storms will come—this is an unavoidable reality of life. But just as eagles use a storm's winds to soar higher, how you navigate life's challenges depends not only on your personal strength in God but also on the people you choose to journey with. While an eagle's natural strength allows it to soar against the wind, an eagle Christian's strength comes from waiting upon the Lord (Isaiah 40:31). Yet, beyond personal spiritual resilience, the people in your boat often determine your safety and success in the storm.

So, as you prepare to dive into this chapter, get ready to discover how to choose relationships that align with your divine vision and empower you to soar. The journey ahead is not just about weathering storms—it's about building a community that helps you rise above them.

Let's dive in.

PAUL VS. JONAH: THE POWER OF THE RIGHT AND WRONG ASSOCIATIONS

The apostle Paul serves as a powerful example of the kind of person you need in your life. When he faced a violent storm at sea, he reassured those around him, saying:

> *"Keep up your courage, because not one of you will be lost; only the ship will be destroyed. Last night an angel of the God to whom I belong and whom I serve stood beside me and said, 'Do not be afraid, Paul. You must stand trial before Caesar; and God has graciously given you the lives of all who sail with you.'" —Acts 27:22-25*

Because of Paul's divine calling and unshakable faith, everyone on board was spared. This story reveals an important truth: the right person, divinely placed in your life, can make all the difference. The right people will uplift and propel you toward your purpose, while the wrong ones can hinder or even derail your destiny.

Now, contrast Paul with Jonah, a prophet who was running from God's will. His presence in the wrong boat brought a deadly storm upon the crew. When the sailors cast lots to determine who was responsible for their misfortune, the lot fell on Jonah:

> *The sea was getting rougher and rougher. So they asked him, "What should we do to you to make the sea calm down for us?" "Pick me up and throw me into the sea," he replied, "and it will become calm. I know that it is my fault that this great storm has come upon you."* —Jonah 1:11-12

Because of Jonah's disobedience, the storm endangered everyone on board. The lesson here is clear: having the wrong person in your skies—or even in your boat—can cause unnecessary turmoil and even derail your destiny.

These two stories illustrate the power of associations. Just as eagles fly in formations that maximize their strength and efficiency, the people you allow to share your journey can either lift you higher or pull you down. Choose wisely, for your associations will shape your flight and determine how high you soar.

Now, let's pause and take a moment to evaluate your relationships. Who is flying with you? As you've just read, your life is a journey, and your relationships are like fellow eagles soaring alongside you. Some are meant to fly with you for a lifetime, others for a season, and some should never have been in your skies at all. You must be intentional about who you allow to share your airspace, for the company you keep can either help you soar higher or weigh you down.

To guide this evaluation, consider these questions:

1) Do the people around you inspire, encourage, and push you toward your God-given purpose?

2) Are they helping you navigate storms, or are they the reason the storms exist?

3) Do they bring wisdom, faith, and vision into your life, or do they bring fear, doubt, and distractions?

This is not just about identifying who belongs in your skies—it's about creating a flock that aligns with your divine vision and empowers you to soar.

As John Stuart Mill said, "One person with vision is greater than the passive force of ninety-nine people who are merely interested in doing or becoming something."[20] This means that it is better to walk alone with God's purpose than for a crowd that hinders your destiny to surround you.

CHOOSING THE RIGHT COMPANY

You were never meant to peck at life's crumbs when God designed you to ride heavenly thermals. Science confirms what Scripture has always declared—eagles soar at altitudes of 10,000 feet while chickens scratch dirt in ten-foot radiuses. This isn't just animal behavior; it's a spiritual law. I've watched too many believers remain earthbound because they took counsel from coop-dwellers. Like the tech executive who nearly abandoned his ministry call when his MBA friends mocked it as "financial suicide"—until he joined an eagles-only mastermind group that prayed him into launching what's now a thriving discipleship network across three continents. History's greatest changemakers understood this principle. Dr. Martin Luther King Jr.'s inner circle didn't include nay-sayers—he surrounded himself with fellow eagles like Andrew Young and John Lewis, who could endure the thin air of racial reconciliation when others gasped for oxygen.

---

20 John Stuart Mill, cited in Gary J. Borgstede, "The Make It Happen Moment: Compound Vision," *FaithWriters*, 18 April 2009, https://www.faithwriters.com/article-details.php?id=97542.

Even Jesus modeled this, spending 90 percent of His time with just twelve men—and only three saw the Transfiguration. Your circle is either giving you altitude or clipping your wings. I've buried too many chicken-hearted Christians who spent their lives clucking about problems rather than mounting up like eagles. The evidence is irrefutable: when a pastor friend I know stopped attending small-minded ministers' meetings and started learning from eagles, her ministry exploded, and she was able to reach the boundaries that God had predetermined her to reach. She stopped taking ministry advice from chickens who'd never left the denominational barnyard.

> *The chickens around you aren't evil; they're just not your species.*

A 2025 study by Harvard researchers Hashim Zaman and Karim Lakhani revealed that workplace sabotage is common, particularly in competitive environments. Their survey of 335 executives found that 71 percent had witnessed managers undermining subordinates to prevent competition.[21] This behavior often stems from fears of losing status or job security. While this study focuses on workplace dynamics, it underscores the broader principle found in 1 Corinthians 15:33: "Do not be misled: 'Bad company corrupts good character.'" The influence of those around us, whether in professional or personal settings, can significantly impact our growth and development.

---

21 Hashim Zaman and Karim R. Lakhani, "What Drives Managers to Sabotage Talented Employees," *Harvard Business School*, 9 Jan. 2025, https://www.library.hbs.edu/working-knowledge/what-drives-managers-to-sabotage-talented-employees.

That businessman sensing a call to fund revivals? He's letting tax consultants talk him out of divine assignments. Here's the eagle truth: you'll never accidentally soar. Every morning, literal eagles choose between riding thermals or perching safely. Today, you're choosing, too—by whom you text, who mentors you, and whose opinions outweigh God's voice. The chickens around you aren't evil; they're just not your species. And while Jesus ate with sinners, He only did ministry with disciples. Your destiny depends on this discernment more than your devotion—because even an eagle becomes chicken-hearted if it refuses to fly with its kind.

THE POWER OF DISCERNMENT IN RELATIONSHIPS

In today's world, trust is not something to be given blindly—it must be earned through consistency and proven commitment. Eagles demonstrate this principle well. Before choosing a mate, a female eagle tests the male's endurance, reliability, and dedication. She drops a twig from great heights, and he must catch it before it reaches the ground. She repeats this process from increasing altitudes until she is convinced of his unwavering commitment. Only then does she accept him.

This same principle applies to modern relationships, business partnerships, and personal growth. Whether in friendships, dating, or professional collaborations, you must be intentional about whom you allow into your life.

- » In relationships, don't rush into deep commitments without observing character, consistency, and true intentions.
- » In business, don't partner with people just because they make promises—test their integrity, reliability, and work ethic first.

» In personal growth, surround yourself with people who uplift and challenge you, not those who drain your energy and distract you from your purpose.

Just like an eagle ensures she aligns herself with a worthy mate, be wise in choosing the people you trust and invest in. Not everyone deserves access to your life—discern first, then commit because who you surround yourself with will either propel you to greatness or hinder your progress.

As you prepare to go places you've never been, achieve things you've never done, and rise to new heights, it is crucial to choose the right people to journey with you. Your association determines your destination. Just as an eagle carefully chooses its mate, you must trust God to connect you with the right people—your destiny helpers. Jesus Himself set an example of divine selection. Before choosing His twelve disciples, He spent twelve hours in prayer (Luke 6:12-16). If Jesus, the Son of God, took time to pray before choosing His inner circle, how much more should we seek God's guidance in our relationships?

Many people carelessly allow anyone into their lives, paying little attention to the impact of these connections. This is a major reason why so many relationships end in pain and disappointment. Your life should not be an open field where people come and go as they please. Every person in your skies must have a God-ordained purpose, or they can become a source of wounds, distractions, and missed opportunities.

As an eagle Christian, you must be intentional. Before allowing anyone into your life, seek God in prayer and ask:

Why is this person here?
What role do they play in my destiny?
Are they sent to help build, or are they here to intentionally or unintentionally break me down?

If you do not understand the purpose of people in your life, you risk mismanaging divine relationships and abusing opportunities God has orchestrated for your growth. Not everyone is meant to stay, and some people should never have been there in the first place.

Your inner circle is either thrusting you toward destiny or dragging you into their drama. Eagles don't flock with chickens—not because they're arrogant but because chickens can't survive at 10,000 feet. Jesus modeled this when He spent an entire night in prayer before handpicking twelve disciples (Luke 6:12-16). Notice He didn't crowdsource opinions or let just anyone into His inner circle. Yet most of us treat our relationships like open-air markets, letting anyone browse the sacred spaces of our calling. I've watched too many anointed people derailed by "friends" who celebrated their dreams but resented their success—like the worship leader whose own choir members secretly sabotaged her record deal because "she was getting too big" or the entrepreneur who lost his marriage because his business partner—a comrade against poverty, not a confidant for life—convinced him family was a distraction.

Your life isn't a public park. Every relationship should pass through the filter of three divine questions: Why is this person here? What kingdom purpose do they serve? Are they holding me back or helping me fly? Some people are scaffolding—meant to stabilize you for a season, then be removed. Others are load-bearing walls, holding up your very foundation. I learned this the hard way when I poured years into mentoring a young preacher, only to realize he wasn't sent to grow with me—he was assigned to drain me. The moment I released, him my ministry doubled.

There are three types of people you'll encounter at every altitude:

1) **Confidants:** They are as rare as diamonds—they love you at your worst and correct you in love. They're the ones who'll tell you when your sermon was off or your attitude stinks, then pray with you until dawn.
2) **Constituents:** They rally around your mission, not your heart. They'll fund your church plant but vanish when you face scandal.
3) **Comrades:** They only stand with you because they hate what you hate. They're the protest buddies who disappear when the marching stops.

Most heartbreak comes from confusing these roles—expecting loyalty from situational allies or mistaking scaffolding for bedrock.

Every person in your life has been assigned either to build you, break you, or reveal what's already inside you. Cherish the rare few who love you at your worst and correct you at your best—these are your confidants. They're the ones who'll sit with you in the ashes of your failure and still call out your destiny when you can't see it. Like Jonathan was to David, your victories don't impress them, and your scars don't scare them. Pour into them relentlessly because, in a world full of transactional relationships, they're the sacred few who mirror Christ's unconditional love.

> *Even the most loyal allies can falter under pressure if their connection to you is situational rather than covenantal.*

Then, there are those drawn to your mission, not your heart—your constituents. They'll fund your vision and celebrate your success, but don't mistake their applause for allegiance. Like the crowds who waved palm branches then shouted, "Crucify Him!" their loyalty lasts only as long as your usefulness. When they walk away—and they will—bless them without bitterness. They were never yours to keep, only divine scaffolding to steady you for a season.

And comrades? They're the situational allies who stand with you only because they hate what you hate. They'll march with you against injustice, then vanish when the protest ends. Like Peter warming himself at the enemy's fire, their commitment burns out when the battle gets personal. Even Peter—the rock of the early church—once traded his bold faith for the comfort of the enemy's fire. But here's the hope: his story didn't end there. After his denial, Jesus restored him (John 21:15-17), and this same Peter later preached at Pentecost, healed the sick, and wrote epistles that still guide us today.

The lesson isn't "Peter failed." It's this: even the most loyal allies can falter under pressure if their connection to you is situational rather than covenantal. Comrades may distance themselves when your mission gets costly—but confidants, like Jesus was to Peter, will help restore you after the rooster crows. Never entrust your heart to a comrade—they're temporary warriors, not lifetime friends.

> *Your relationships can either elevate you or destroy you.*

Here's the eagle test: if you removed your title, your money, and your influence, who would still speak to you? Those are your confidants. The rest are either assignments or distractions. Stop letting chickens vote on your flight path. The moment you grasp this truth, your relationships will never be the same—this is the discernment that separates eagles from chickens.

Moses had Aaron and Hur holding his arms up in battle—but he also had to bury the generation that murmured in the wilderness. David had a Jonathan, but he also had to dismiss the Ahithophels who betrayed him. Even Jesus kept His inner circle small—twelve disciples, three confidants, and one beloved. Your relationships will make or break your destiny. You have a divine assignment—so stop letting just anyone board your ark because some have been assigned to sink it! Just like not every bird in your airspace is your wingman; some are circling to distract you.

If you fail to discern who should stay and who should leave, you will waste time, energy, and emotions on people who were never meant to be permanent. If you confide in a comrade, you will face betrayal. If you expect a constituent to stay, you will be disappointed. If you neglect a confidant, you will lose a valuable gift. Your relationships can either elevate you or destroy you. Choose wisely, discern carefully, and seek God's wisdom before allowing anyone in.

ASSOCIATIONS DETERMINE YOUR DESTINATION

Just as Paul's presence led to salvation and Jonah's presence brought turmoil, the people in your life will either propel you toward your purpose or pull you into unnecessary struggles or turbulence. The relationships you cultivate are not insignificant—they play a crucial role in shaping your destiny. You may practice the following as a guide for choosing your associations wisely:

1) **Pray for divine connections:** Seek God's guidance in surrounding yourself with people who will uplift and support your purpose, while removing those who hinder your growth.

2) **Evaluate your current relationships:** Are you soaring alongside eagles, or are you grounded with those who limit your potential? The trajectory of your future depends on the company you keep.

3) **Discern before you allow access:** Not everyone is meant to walk your journey with you. Some relationships are divine connections that will elevate you, while others are distractions that will hold you back.

Life is like a flight, and the people you allow in your skies will influence whether you rise, struggle, or fall. Sometimes, wisdom requires loving certain individuals from a distance—not out of resentment but for the sake of your purpose.

As a believer called to soar, you must be intentional about your associations. You were designed to fly with fellow eagles—those who encourage your vision, sharpen your faith, and push you toward greatness. Beware of those who lack vision, drain your energy, and hinder your ability to soar.

> Accommodating the wrong person in your life is a great danger to the fulfillment of your destiny.
> —Tessy Tanyi

But soaring with the right flock is only part of the journey. To truly rise above life's storms and walk in your divine purpose, you must also develop the eagle's vision—a spiritual insight that allows you to perceive beyond the natural and into the supernatural.

In the next chapter, we will dive into the art of sharpening your spiritual awareness, aligning your focus with God's perspective, and discerning His will in every season. Just as an eagle's sharp eyesight enables it to detect prey from incredible heights, your spiritual perception will help you recognize opportunities, avoid pitfalls, and navigate life with divine wisdom.

So, as you turn the page, prepare to elevate your perspective and see through the eyes of an eagle Christian. The journey ahead is not just about who you soar with—it's about how you see.

> Show me your flock,
> and I'll show you your future.
> Eagles don't rehearse with chickens.
> Your inner circle is your outer destiny.
> —Tessy Tanyi

CHAPTER 12

THE EAGLE'S GAZE

Developing Spiritual Perception

> "The LORD said to Abram after Lot had parted from him, 'Look around from where you are, to the north and south, to the east and west. All the land that you see I will give to you and your offspring forever.'"
> —Genesis 13:14-15

> How far you see determines how far you will go.
> —Tessy Tanyi

In a world that moves at lightning speed, many of us are conditioned to trust what we see at first glance. We make decisions based on surface appearances—the immediate benefits of a job offer, the outward charm of a person, the seeming security of a financial investment—without pausing to look deeper. But there is a difference between eyes that look and eyes that see.

An eagle's eyes are one of its greatest strengths. While humans may see details from a few hundred feet away, an eagle can lock onto its prey from miles above, cutting through the haze of distance and distraction. It doesn't just see what is right now—it perceives what could be.

I didn't always have the eyes of an eagle. For years, I made choices based on what seemed good at the moment. I trusted people who talked the right way but had the wrong motives. I pursued opportunities that glittered like gold but crumbled like sand. I mistook comfort for purpose and security for calling. But then, God allowed me to walk through a season where my natural sight failed me. A promising door I had eagerly walked through turned out to be a dead end. Relationships I thought were divinely orchestrated shattered before my eyes. I had been looking, but I had not been seeing. It was in that season of disappointment that God opened my spiritual eyes. He reminded me of how God told Abram—after Lot left—to *look*. Not just glance, not just observe, but to truly see what was possible beyond his present moment. God didn't give Abram the land he merely stood on—He gave him the land he saw.

I realized then that vision is the currency of destiny. If you only see what is in front of you, you will never reach beyond where you are.

DEVELOPING THE EAGLE'S GAZE

Developing spiritual perception means training yourself to see beyond the natural:

» Seeing people beyond their words—Not everyone who speaks well means well.

» Seeing opportunities beyond comfort—Sometimes, the hardest path is the right one.

» Seeing trials beyond the pain—What looks like an obstacle may be a divine setup for transformation.

Like Abram, God calls us to lift our eyes—not to what is convenient, but to what He has prepared. Like an eagle, we must rise above the noise and distractions of this world and fix our gaze on what truly matters. I once walked blindly into choices that led me nowhere. But now, with the sharpened vision that only comes from God, I see what I could not see before. And that has made all the difference. I'll never forget the season when my vision was put to the test. A job opportunity came my way—one that boasted prestige, a generous salary, and all the outward signs of success. At first glance, it seemed like the perfect fit, a once-in-a-lifetime chance to elevate my career. But deep down, something felt off.

I remember whispering a simple prayer: "God, this looks ideal, but I need Your eyes to truly see." As I pressed in, seeking His guidance, I began to notice things I had overlooked. The work environment was toxic, the role demanded compromises that clashed with my values, and the relentless hours would strip me of time with my family and my true calling. What appeared to be a golden opportunity was, in reality, a beautifully disguised trap. Saying no felt risky, but I chose to walk away. In time, God opened a financial door—one that not only aligned with my purpose but allowed me to thrive without

> *Eyes that look are common, but eyes that see are rare.*

sacrificing what mattered most. That experience reshaped my understanding of vision. True spiritual perception isn't just about recognizing what's directly in front of you; it's about discerning what God is leading you toward.

Are you looking? Or are you truly seeing? I have often heard the saying that eyes that look are common, but eyes that see are rare.

Just as an eagle can pinpoint a single fish in an endless sea, your spiritual perception allows you to recognize God's presence and purpose in every situation. It's about looking beyond the obvious—past fleeting rewards, momentary ease, and surface-level assurances. It's about tuning your vision to God's promises and believing that His plans far exceed what your natural eyes can grasp.

In this chapter, we'll dive into how to cultivate the eagle's gaze—how to sharpen your spiritual insight, align your perspective with God's, and view life through the lens of faith. Because when you begin to see as God sees, you'll walk boldly into the destiny He has already prepared for you.

When God was preparing to fulfill His promise to Abraham, separation from Lot became necessary. Abraham, obeying God's call, gave Lot the choice of land—an opportunity Lot saw as a golden chance to secure the best for himself:

> *Lot took a long look at the fertile plains of the Jordan Valley in the direction of Zoar. . . . The whole area was well watered everywhere, like the garden of the LORD or the beautiful land of Egypt. (This was before the LORD destroyed Sodom and Gomorrah.) Lot chose for himself the whole Jordan Valley to the east of them.* —Genesis 13:10-11 (NLT)

Lot carefully examined the economic and material benefits of the land, but he failed to see its spiritual cost. The land was fertile, water was abundant, and everything seemed promising—but he overlooked the moral corruption of Sodom and Gomorrah. His shortsightedness led to destruction, costing him everything, including his wife and wealth. In contrast, Abraham walked by faith, not by sight. He trusted God's promise over human reasoning and was ultimately blessed beyond measure.

Lot's mistake is still common today and reminds us of the danger of short-sighted choices. Many people choose careers only for financial gain, ignoring whether they align with their purpose. Some enter relationships based on attraction and convenience, without discerning character and values. Still, others make decisions based on immediate comfort, rather than long-term spiritual impact.

We live in a world where instant gratification is prioritized, where people choose the "greenest" path to avoid struggle, opposition, and risk. However, true spiritual discernment requires seeing beyond the obvious—understanding that not every opportunity is from God, and not everything that looks good is actually good. Many people live their lives reacting to what is visible, never realizing that true vision comes from seeing beyond the surface.

> *The same God who gave eagles unmatched vision will upgrade your sight.*

SEEING WITH HEAVEN'S PERSPECTIVE

High above the chaos of the earth, eagles lock onto their target with razor-sharp vision—unshaken by distractions, undeterred by distance. This isn't just biological superiority; it's a divine blueprint for how we're called to live. In a world drowning in noise, God invites you to trade human sight for *spiritual perception*—to see the unseen and claim what others miss.

Cultivating the Eagle's Vision

1) **Pray First, Move Second:** Abraham didn't stake his future on Canaan's barren surface; he saw it through God's promise (Genesis 13:14-15). Like him, your breakthroughs begin when you kneel before you leap. *Prayer Prompt:* "Lord, rip away the veil of my limited sight. Show me what You see."

2) **Act on Revelation, Not Just Observation:** An eagle doesn't circle prey forever—it strikes when clarity comes. When God illuminates your path, hesitation is disobedience. Remember Peter walking on water: his feet sank only when he switched his gaze from Christ to the waves (Matthew 14:30). *Prayer prompt:* "Lord, give me the courage to act when You speak. Help me recognize the difference between waiting in wisdom and hesitating in fear. Keep my eyes fixed on You, so that when You reveal the next step, I move—not with doubt, but with bold trust. Teach me to walk by faith, not by sight, and to strike when clarity comes."

3) **See Beyond the Temporary:** Lot chose Sodom's lush valleys but inherited its judgment (Genesis 13:10-13). His eyes saw prosperity; his spirit missed the poison. He chose the lush valleys of Sodom, drawn by what looked good at the moment (Genesis 13:10–13). But what his eyes called prosperity, his spirit failed to test—and he inherited destruction instead of blessing. His decision was rooted in sight, not in discernment.

Every opportunity that looks promising isn't from God. So, test it: "Will this draw me closer to God's throne or Satan's table?" *Prayer Prompt:* "Lord, help me not to be led by what looks good, but by what is truly from You. Open my spiritual eyes to see beyond surface-level opportunities. Teach me to test every door, every relationship, and every decision through the lens of Your Word. If it draws me away from You, give me the strength to walk away. I want to choose Your presence over any temporary promise."

4) **Train Your Eyes on Scripture:** God's promises are lenses that correct spiritual blindness. When life feels unclear, it's not a new plan you need—it's a clearer perspective. Scripture sharpens your vision. David—a shepherd turned king—knew this when he wrote, "Your word is a lamp to my feet and a light to my path" (Psalm 119:105, ESV). **Write down His pledges.** Declare them daily. Repeat them until what you see with your eyes matches what He has spoken to your spirit. *Prayer Prompt:* "Father, train my eyes to see through the lens of Your Word. When my sight is clouded by doubt, distraction, or fear, remind me of Your promises. Let Your truth correct my vision and guide my steps. Help me to not just read Your Word—but believe it, declare it, and live by it until my vision aligns fully with Yours."

5) **Surround Yourself with Seers:** Eagles don't take flight lessons from chickens. If you're called to soar, you can't afford to stay grounded by small vision or by those who can't see what God is doing in you. When Elijah felt isolated and discouraged, God reminded him he wasn't alone—there were 7,000 others who hadn't bowed to Baal (1 Kings 19:18). You're not the only

one pursuing purpose. But to thrive, you need to walk with people who see what God is doing—people who speak fire, carry faith, and live with vision. Find your tribe of fire-eyed believers. Surround yourself with those who sharpen your spirit, not shrink your calling. *Prayer Prompt:* "Lord, help me recognize the voices You've placed around me for strength and clarity. Lead me to those who see with spiritual eyes and speak with kingdom perspective. Remove the voices that distract, and draw me into community with those who will call out my purpose and stir my faith."

The difference between victory and disaster often hinges on one question: *are you seeing with natural eyes or spiritual insight?* Lot's wife looked back and became a monument of salt (Genesis 19:26). Gehazi saw Naaman's gifts and lost his mantle (2 Kings 5:20-27). Yet Caleb saw giants through God's faithfulness and claimed his mountain (Numbers 13:30).

Pause now and ask yourself:

» Do I see my future through God's promises or my present circumstances?
» Am I settling for earthbound vision when heaven offers eagle-eyed clarity?
» Who in my life sharpens my spiritual sight—and who dulls it?

This isn't about positive thinking. It's about prophetic seeing—the kind that made Elisha spot angelic armies before his servant did (2 Kings 6:17). The same God who gave eagles unmatched vision will upgrade your sight. But you must choose: will you keep scratching the dirt with chickens, or will you mount up and see what others call impossible?

> God has placed a unique purpose and vision inside you, but how far you go depends on how far you can see.
> —Tessy Tanyi

A VISION BEYOND SIGHT

In today's world, logic, experience, and tangible evidence often guide decisions. Yet spiritual vision operates differently—it calls for faith, the ability to perceive what the natural eye cannot yet see. Scripture declares: "Now faith is the substance of things hoped for, the evidence of things not seen" (Hebrews 11:1, NKJV). Faith, then, is divine sight—a lens that reveals God's promises before they come to pass.

History's most impactful achievers—whether in faith, business, or personal transformation—share one trait: they see the future before it unfolds. They are not limited by their circumstances but are guided by a higher reality. In contrast, many remain stuck because they rely solely on their physical sight. They focus on their struggles, limitations, and obstacles, missing the greater destiny God has prepared for them. True progress begins when we shift our gaze from what is visible to what is believed. After all, faith does not deny reality—it sees beyond it.

Many people live in spiritual blindness without realizing it. While physical eyes perceive the world, spiritual eyes reveal destiny. Those who only look at their surroundings remain trapped in confusion, doubt, and uncertainty. But those who learn to see through God's eyes gain clarity, purpose, and unshakable confidence.

History's greatest leaders, innovators, and pioneers had one thing in common: they saw the impossible before it became possible. Your spiritual vision shapes your future—how far you can see determines how far you can go. Let's explore biblical examples of those who saw beyond the natural:

1) **Noah—Vision Beyond the Visible:** While the world lived in rebellion, Noah saw a coming judgment—and a promise of salvation. Others mocked him, but his faith compelled him to build an ark. Because he saw what God revealed, he saved his family and changed history (Genesis 6:11-22).

2) **Moses—Seeing Deliverance Before It Came:** The Israelites saw only slavery; Moses saw freedom. Though Pharaoh's power seemed unshakable, Moses fixed his eyes on God's promise. His spiritual sight led a nation out of bondage (Exodus 3:7-10).

3) **David—A Champion's Perspective:** When Israel trembled before Goliath, David saw an opportunity for God's glory. Others saw an unbeatable giant; he saw a defeated foe. His faith-filled vision brought victory (1 Samuel 17).

4) **Paul—From Blindness to Revelation:** Saul the persecutor became Paul the apostle when his spiritual eyes were opened. The scales that fell from his eyes symbolized his transformation—from religious blindness to divine purpose (Acts 9:17-18).

Your vision sets your course, and your course determines your destiny.

If you only see obstacles, they'll keep you trapped. But if you develop spiritual sight, you'll break every barrier. Like an eagle soaring above the storm, fix your gaze on God's promises and move forward with bold faith.

What do you see?

Your answer will determine how far you go.

APOSTLE SAMUEL OGBONMWAN: THE SEER WHO CHANGED HISTORY

In a world where many with perfect vision remain directionless, Apostle Samuel Ogbonmwan's life stands as a divine paradox—a man physically blind yet spiritually sighted who redefined what it means to truly see. His story shatters the myth that limitations determine destiny, proving instead that faith is the lens through which God rewrites human potential.

At fourteen, young Samuel's world went dark—but where most would see an ending, God planted a genesis. While many today wander with 20/20 vision yet live purposelessly, Ogbonmwan chose to see like Moses at the burning bush: not the barrenness of his condition but the unconsumed fire of divine calling. His journey echoes Paul's transformation:

> The eagles of destiny don't fly by sight— they soar on thermals of revelation.

"Though outwardly we are wasting away, yet inwardly we are being renewed day by day" (2 Corinthians 4:16).

Armed with a bell, a Bible, and boundless faith, Ogbonmwan turned Benin City's idol-worshiping strongholds into harvest fields. At a time when Christianity faced fierce resistance, he:

- » **Pioneered Indigenous gospel music**, using Benin-language lyrics to disarm cultural barriers
- » **Scriptured without sight**, memorizing and expounding on God's Word with supernatural precision

- » **Confronted royalty**, preaching before the Oba of Benin's court—an unthinkable feat for a "disabled" man. His ministry birthed over 200 churches globally, proving that when God opens spiritual eyes, physical circumstances bow.

But before the legacy came the breaking. Behind every bold move was a man who had to wrestle with despair—and rise. Three times he tried to end his life; on the third, heaven intervened. His darkest hour birthed his brightest revelation:

- » Breakthrough is often born at the breaking point.
- » God's greatest purposes are hidden in life's cruelest turns.
- » True visionaries aren't just dreamers—they're forged in the fires of despair.

Like Joseph in the pit or Jonah in the fish, Ogbonmwan's pain became his pulpit.

Honorary doctorates, royal recognitions, and transcontinental impact crowned his journey—but his real trophies were the souls he ushered into light. He embodied Isaiah's prophecy: "I will lead the blind by ways they have not known" (Isaiah 42:16).

THE PROPHETIC CHALLENGE

Ogbonmwan's life demands we ask:

1) **What's your excuse?** If a blind man could memorize Scripture, what's stopping you from studying it?
2) **Where's your focus?** He saw souls, not setbacks—are you fixated on obstacles or opportunities?
3) **When will you act?** The Acts of the Apostles was written because they *moved*—what's your next faith step?

The eagles of destiny don't fly by sight—they soar on thermals of revelation. Storms will come, but like Ogbonmwan, your battles will be won not with eyes but with insight. The question remains: will you, like this sightless seer, dare to perceive what God has already prepared? Your future isn't hidden in what you see—it's revealed in what you *believe*.

"Walk by faith, not by sight" (2 Corinthians 5:7, ESV). This is your divine invitation—not to imitate his story but to awaken your own. The world doesn't need another Ogbonmwan; it needs you to rise, armed with the unique vision God has placed in your spirit. The question isn't whether the world is waiting, but whether you'll dare to step into the story only you can write.

In the next chapter, we will uncover the enemy's tactics, equip you to stand firm in your faith, and show you how to fight from a position of victory. You'll discover how to put on the full armor of God, recognize spiritual attacks, and break through every obstacle that tries to hold you back.

So, as you prepare to turn the page, get ready to step onto the battlefield with confidence and clarity. This journey is not just about soaring—it's about overcoming.

Victory awaits.

> What you focus on fuels you.
> Hell knows this—
> which is why it keeps handing you
> binoculars for your wounds
> while God holds out a telescope
> for your destiny.
> —Tessy Tanyi

CHAPTER 13

RISE ABOVE THE BATTLE

How to Fight Like a Victor, not a Victim

> "Is it at your command that the eagle mounts up And makes his nest on high [in an inaccessible place]?"
> "On the cliff he dwells and remains [securely], Upon the point of the rock and the inaccessible stronghold.
> "From there he spies out the prey; His eyes see it from far away."
> Job 39:27-29 (AMP)

My mother once spoke words that have stayed with me my entire life: "Tessy, an open door invites the wrong people in, and when they enter, they will steal what matters most—your joy, your peace, your very soul." At the time, I thought she was simply teaching me to lock the house at night. But as my faith deepened, I realized she was revealing a powerful spiritual truth: some battles aren't fought with locks and keys—they're fought in the unseen, in the mind, in the spirit.

The enemy doesn't attack where you're strong—he slithers in where you're unguarded. Leave your mind unprotected, and he will pillage your faith, sabotage your confidence, and distort your purpose. That's why the eagle doesn't nest in the open valley—she ascends to the heights, positioning herself beyond the reach of predators. And so must we.

I learned this the hard way. There was a season when I fought with nothing but my own strength—my emotions, my arguments, my sheer willpower. I thought if I just pushed harder, defended louder, or outworked the opposition, I could win. But all it did

> *My job wasn't to claw my way to triumph; it was to stand firm in what was already mine.*

was drain me. I was swinging at air, battling spiritual forces with flesh and bone. I was fighting from the low ground when I was called to rise.

The breakthrough came when I stopped wrestling in my own power and took my place on the Rock—when I traded my frustration for faith, my striving for surrender. Because true victory isn't found in the scramble of the valley—it's claimed from the summit.

So, tell me—where have you been fighting from? The vulnerable open field? Or the unshakable heights? **It's time to ascend.**

It wasn't until I grasped the reality of spiritual warfare that I stopped struggling and started dominating. No more knee-jerk reactions—no more fear, no more frantic frustration. Instead, I learned to engage with precision, wisdom, and divine strategy.

The enemy's favorite playground? The mind. His tactics? Whispered lies. Doubt to paralyze you. Fear to shrink you. Insecurity to make you forget who you are. But when I flooded my thoughts with truth—when I declared God's promises like weapons instead of pleading like a victim—the game changed.

Here's the revelation that rewired everything: I wasn't fighting for victory—I was fighting *from* victory. Christ had already secured the win. My job wasn't to claw my way to triumph; it was to stand firm in what was already mine.

Let me be clear: success doesn't wander into open, unguarded lives. It's seized by those who:

1) Recognize the war (because ignorance is the first casualty).
2) Prepare like a strategist (full armor on, Spirit-empowered).
3) Advance like a conqueror (not in panic but in authority).

The question isn't if you're in a battle—it's where you're positioned in it. Are you scrambling in the dirt, or are you standing on the Rock, declaring the enemy's defeat?

The higher your posture, the clearer your victory.

So, tell me—how's your positioning?

In this chapter, we're going on the offensive. No more playing defense, no more reacting in fear—just unshakable strategy, razor-sharp discernment, and unstoppable spiritual authority.

You'll learn:

» How to expose the enemy's playbook—because you can't defeat what you don't recognize.
» How to fortify your mind and spirit—building a defense so strong that doubt and fear can't breach it.
» How to wield spiritual weapons that actually win wars—not flesh and blood but divine power that crushes strongholds.

Like the eagle, you were made for the heights. The higher your perspective, the clearer your victory. This isn't about striving in your own strength—it's about standing firm in a triumph that's already been won. So, I ask you again: will you fight like the warrior you were created to be? Or will you cower on the sidelines while the enemy steals what's yours?

The battle is real. But so is your victory. Now, rise—and take your place in it.

THE ENEMY'S PRIMARY BATTLEFIELD

The enemy's most strategic attacks don't come through circumstances—they come through your thoughts. This is where battles are won or lost. Satan knows that whoever controls your mind controls your destiny.

Satan's primary strategies are:

- » **Doubt:** He makes you question God's promises and His goodness.
- » **Discouragement:** He makes you focus on your struggles instead of God's power.
- » **Diversion:** He distracts you with worldly pleasures and meaningless pursuits.
- » **Self-Condemnation:** He makes you feel like a failure, keeping you from moving forward.
- » **Laziness/Procrastination:** He delays you from fulfilling your God-given purpose.

But you were never meant to fight on his turf.

Eagles don't wrestle in the dirt—they dominate from the skies. And like them, victorious believers don't engage the enemy on his terms. Instead, they:

1) **Reclaim their thoughts.** As an eagle, you must saturate your mind with truth.

> *"We demolish arguments and every pretension that sets itself up against the knowledge of God, and we take captive every thought to make it obedient to Christ."*
> —2 Corinthians 10:5

Silence every lie with Scripture using these three "pills:"

<u>The Thought Filter</u>: "Whatever is true, whatever is noble, whatever is right, whatever is pure, whatever is lovely, whatever is admirable—if anything is excellent or praiseworthy—think about such things" (Philippians 4:8). If a thought does not fit these criteria, reject it immediately!

<u>The Thought Captor</u>: "We take captive every thought to make it obedient to Christ" (2 Corinthians 10:5). This means you have the authority to reject any thought that does not align with God's Word.

<u>The Enemy Resister</u>: "Away from me, Satan! For it is written: 'Worship the Lord your God, and serve him only.' Then the devil left him, and angels came and attended him" (Matthew 4:10-11). Satan will not leave you until you actively resist him!

2) **Rise above the noise.** As an eagle, you must reject fear's narrative and starve distractions vying for your attention.

> *"Do not conform to the pattern of this world, but be transformed by the renewing of your mind."*
> —Romans 12:2

3) **Operate from higher ground.** As an eagle, prayer is your altitude, and discernment is your advantage.

> *"Set your minds on things above, not on earthly things."*
> —Colossians 3:2

4) **Shift from defense to dominance.** Stop reacting; start decreeing. Don't fight for the victory—enforce it.
> *"Resist the devil, and he will flee from you."*
> —James 4:7

CRUSHING THE ENEMY'S MIND GAMES

The serpent is powerless in the skies as he slithers on the ground, just as Satan becomes impotent when you rise above his mental strongholds. His entire kingdom depends on one strategy: controlling your thoughts to hijack your destiny. While many believers struggle with negative thinking, fear, and self-doubt, they fail to realize—these aren't random attacks. This is war.

> *The battlefield is your mind—but the victory is already yours. Now, take your place in it.*

From Eden to today, the devil's playbook hasn't changed:
1) **The Doubt Injection**: *"Did God really say?"* (Genesis 3:1)
2) **The Identity Eraser**: *"You're not good enough."*
3) **The Fear Bomb**: *"What if you fail?"*
4) **The Delay Trap**: *"Someday . . . but not now."*
5) **The Condemnation Loop**: *"You're too messed up for God's plan."*

These lies keep believers stranded in mental bondage, preventing them from ever stepping into their God-given authority. But

Jesus revealed the counterattack. When Satan came at Jesus with lies, Jesus didn't:
» Debate the devil
» Overanalyze the temptation
» Entertain the thought for even a second

You need to use the same battle plan Jesus used. He nuked the attack with the Word: *"It is written...."* (Matthew 4:4-10).

Your Three-Step Battle Plan for Mental Dominion

1) **Recognize the lie** (expose the enemy's strategy): Before a thought takes root, interrogate it:
   > *Does this align with God's Word?*
   > *Does this produce faith or fear?*
   > *Is this thought leading me toward or away from my purpose?*

2) **Reject it immediately** (no neutral ground): You wouldn't let a thief into your house—why let a thief into your mind?
   > Fear? *"God has not given me a spirit of fear!"* (2 Timothy 1:7)
   > Doubt? *"I can do all things through Christ!"* (Philippians 4:13)
   > Condemnation? *"I am fearfully and wonderfully made!"* (Psalm 139:14)

3) **Replace it with the truth** (launch a counterstrike): Your mind is like a battlefield—if you don't occupy it with truth, the enemy will occupy it with lies.
   > Daily Scripture bombardment (Write, speak, memorize)
   > Worship as warfare (Break strongholds with praise)
   > Prayer as positioning (Elevate above the enemy's reach)

Eagles don't fight snakes on the ground—they lift off and strike from above. You have the same advantage to:

- » **See from God's perspective** (Colossians 3:2)
- » **Strike with precision** (2 Corinthians 10:5)
- » **Dominate, don't debate** (James 4:7)

Your mind is the control center of your destiny. Take it back—and watch the enemy flee because—praise God—what was stolen in Eden has been restored at Calvary! Through Christ, you've been given back full dominion—but now it's time to enforce it. The enemy doesn't surrender territory willingly—you must take it back by force (Matthew 11:12). This battle starts in your mind because Satan knows if he controls your thoughts, he controls your destiny. That's why Romans 12:2 roars: "Be transformed by the renewing of your mind!" This isn't passive—it's a war cry for mental revolution. You're not some helpless sparrow pecking at crumbs of doubt—you're an eagle, wired to soar above the storm! So, stop letting the enemy's lies nest in your mind. Tear them down with truth. Refuse to entertain fear, reject every whisper of condemnation, and command your thought realm to align with heaven's decree. The same power that raised Christ from the dead lives in you (Romans 8:11)—so stop begging and start declaring. The victory's already yours—now enforce it, occupy it, and live like the conqueror you are!

> *"Submit yourselves, then, to God. Resist the devil, and he will flee from you."*
> —James 4:7

If you're not currently walking in the fullness of your God-given purpose, recognize this as a clear sign: the enemy has gained a strategic advantage in your thought life. But this moment marks your turning point. Victory isn't something you hope for in the future; it's your present inheritance waiting to be claimed. Far too many believers suffer unnecessary defeats, passively waiting for God to move when He has already equipped them with everything needed for triumph.

Your true identity shatters every lie of the enemy: You are not a helpless victim but a trained warrior. You are not vulnerable prey but a proven conqueror (Romans 8:37). You are never powerless, for you possess the full arsenal of heaven (2 Corinthians 10:4). This is your spiritual DNA in Christ.

Your battle strategy unfolds with precision: First, fortify your mind as the primary battleground—your thoughts determine your territory, so guard them with relentless vigilance. Second, unleash the offensive power of Scripture, speaking God's Word as the living, active weapon it is (Isaiah 55:11). Third, engage in strategic spiritual warfare through targeted prayer and worship—they aren't religious activities but direct assaults on enemy strongholds. Fourth, take an authoritative stand in your God-given dominion, moving from defense to decisive decree (Luke 10:19).

> *As an eagle believer, you're called to rise above ground-level struggles and enforce Christ's finished work.*

Understand this spiritual reality: the enemy responds only to violent faith (Matthew 11:12), not polite petitions. As an eagle believer, you're called to rise above ground-level struggles and enforce Christ's finished work. The victory is secured—now live in it. This is your divine moment to stand unshakable. As Romans 16:20 declares, "The God of peace will soon crush Satan under your feet," but you must take your position for this promise to activate. The question remains: will you remain passive or rise to your prophetic purpose?

Never engage the enemy on his terms. Like the eagle, shift the battlefield—ascend in prayer and watch God dismantle what you could never overcome in your own strength.

Many believers find themselves spiritually drained, fighting endless battles because they're combatting the wrong enemies the wrong way. Hosea 4:6 reveals the sobering truth: "My people are destroyed for lack of knowledge." What appears as mere ignorance is actually the enemy's most effective trap. When you don't understand your royal inheritance in Christ, you'll waste energy fighting flesh-and-blood battles with human wisdom and weak weapons. But when you reposition the conflict into the heavenly realm—bringing it before God's throne—victory ceases to be a possibility; it's a guaranteed outcome.

> *The enemy's power exists only where your knowledge of Christ's authority ends.*

THE EAGLE'S BRILLIANT MANEUVER

Consider the deadly serpent on the ground. It's a ruthless predator, stealing eggs and suffocating life. But the eagle knows a secret; it never fights the snake in the dirt. Instead, it lifts the serpent into the sky, where gravity renders it helpless. In midair, the snake's fangs become meaningless, its coils useless, its threat neutralized. One strategic shift in altitude transforms the entire battle.

This is your spiritual warfare model:

1) **Exchange struggle for soaring**: The enemy wants you entangled in earthly conflicts, emotional turmoil, and human reasoning. Refuse to engage at that level. Elevate every battle through prayer, worship, and God's Word (Ephesians 6:12).

2) **Appeal to heaven's court**: Your case belongs before the righteous Judge (Revelation 12:10). His rulings override every earthly plot against you.

3) **Watch demonic strongholds crumble**: What appears invincible in the natural realm is laughably weak in the spiritual dimension. Even demons shudder in the presence of God's glory (James 2:19).

This is your divine battle plan:

1) **Pray with authority**: Move beyond begging to boldly declaring heaven's verdicts from your position in Christ (Hebrews 4:16).

2) **Worship as warfare**: Praise isn't just singing—it's a tactical strike that sends enemy forces into confusion (2 Chronicles 20:22).

3) **Command, don't converse**: Follow Jesus's example: He never debated the devil; He demolished him with Scripture (Matthew 4:10).

The enemy's power exists only where your knowledge of Christ's authority ends. So, spread your wings, eagle of God! Carry every attack, every lie, every threat into the throne room—and watch as what was meant to break you becomes broken before you.

> *"But thanks be to God, who always leads us as captives in Christ's triumphal procession."*
> —2 Corinthians 2:14

You exist in two dimensions simultaneously—the visible natural world and the invisible spiritual realm. This dual citizenship changes everything about how we engage in battle. Too many believers exhaust themselves swinging at shadows, trying to overcome spiritual strongholds with natural weapons that always fall short. But true victory—dominion-level victory—is only won when we shift the fight to the spiritual realm where Christ already reigns supreme.

An eagle never makes the fatal mistake of fighting a snake on the ground. With piercing vision, it assesses the battlefield, then does something revolutionary—it lifts conflict into the skies, changing the entire theater of war. This single tactical decision renders the serpent powerless.

This is your divine warfare strategy—When you take your battles before heaven's courtroom, three supernatural transactions occur:

1) **The Blood of Jesus silences every accusation**—No charge can stand against you when heaven's perfect Defense Attorney pleads your case (Revelation 12:11).
2) **Demonic strongholds crumble**—In God's presence, every enemy plot unravels (Psalm 91:1).
3) **Victory shifts from potential to permanent**—You're not struggling to win but enforcing what Christ already secured (Colossians 2:15).

Spiritual warfare isn't about learning how to fight—it's about knowing *where* to fight. The eagle doesn't defeat the snake by becoming a better ground fighter; it wins by changing altitudes.

Likewise, your breakthrough comes when you stop wrestling in the flesh and start reigning in the spirit.

You're not fighting *for* victory—you're fighting *from* victory. When this truth grips your spirit, you become unstoppable. Like the eagle mounting up on thermals of God's presence, you'll rise above every attack, every lie, every limitation. The enemy has no counter for a believer who knows their position in Christ and wages war from heaven's throne room.

YOUR CALL TO ARMS

Are you still battling on the enemy's terms? Still trying to out-argue, out-work, or out-worry your spiritual opposition? It's time for a radical repositioning. Anchor your mind in Christ the way an eagle secures its nest on impregnable cliffs. Wrap yourself in the armor of God, not as a desperate defense but as the uniform of your royal authority.

This isn't about survival—it's about *dominion*. You carry resurrection power (Ephesians 1:19-20), wield angelic assistance (Hebrews 1:14), and operate under heaven's full backing. When you step onto the battlefield equipped with these realities, you don't just endure storms—you *ride them* to new altitudes of victory.

True warriors understand that lasting victory requires more than weapons—it demands *strength*. An eagle doesn't soar without first nourishing itself. In our next chapter, we'll explore how to fortify your whole being—body, mind, and spirit—for maximum spiritual impact. You'll discover:

» How vitality fuels spiritual endurance
» The mind-renewal practices that make you attack-proof

» Spiritual disciplines that turn ordinary believers into supernatural threats to darkness

This isn't just another teaching—it's your training manual for reigning in life. Turn the page with holy anticipation. Your transformation from battle-weary to battle-ready starts now. The eagles are rising—will you be among them?

"But those who wait on the LORD Shall renew their strength; They shall mount up with wings like eagles."
—Isaiah 40:31

> The battle isn't for victory—
> it's from victory.
> Stop fighting like a soldier trying to win.
> Start enforcing like a king
> who already has.
> —Tessy Tanyi

CHAPTER 14

FEEDING THE EAGLE WITHIN

*Strengthening Your
Spirit and Mind*

"Now the Berean Jews were of more noble character than those in Thessalonica, for they received the message with great eagerness and examined the Scriptures every day to see if what Paul said was true."
—Acts 17:11

This verse vividly illustrates the depth of discernment and the intentional pursuit of truth that characterizes an eagle Christian. Just as an eagle rises above distractions and uses its sharp vision to focus on what is valuable, the Bereans displayed spiritual clarity and diligence. They didn't blindly accept teachings but examined the Scriptures daily to verify the truth for themselves.

In today's fast-paced world, where information is abundant and easily accessible, the real challenge isn't finding truth—it's discerning it. With countless voices, ideologies, and perspectives competing for our attention, it's easy to become confused or led astray. But an eagle Christian is not a passive consumer. Like the Bereans, we are called to seek divine revelation, distinguish truth from deception, and cultivate personal spiritual strength.

Neither the Bereans nor eagle Christians settle for surface-level knowledge. Both are active seekers, consuming only what is fresh, nourishing, and aligned with God's Word. Just as an eagle refuses to eat what is dead or decayed, we, too, must reject spiritual complacency and pursue what sustains our growth and sharpens our discernment.

Now that you have broken free from the limitations of a "chicken mentality" and embraced your identity as an eagle Christian, you stand on the edge of new heights, wings stretched, ready to soar into the fullness of your destiny. You've learned to embrace the wilderness, trust God in the storms, and discern His voice above the noise of the world. However, before you launch into the sky, there is a vital step you must take: you must nourish your spirit and mind.

The higher you soar, the more strength you will need. Just as an eagle must carefully choose its food to maintain its power and agility, you must be intentional about what you feed your spirit and mind. One of the greatest threats to spiritual growth is stagnation—settling for old revelations, becoming too comfortable, and failing to pursue fresh wisdom from God. If you desire to keep soaring, you must be mindful of what you allow to nourish your soul and shape your life.

In this chapter, we'll explore how to cultivate a lifestyle of spiritual and mental nourishment that equips you to thrive. From feeding on God's Word to renewing your mind and strengthening your discernment, you will discover how to develop the endurance, resilience, and clarity needed to soar higher than ever before.

THE POWER OF INTENTIONAL GROWTH

In our hyperconnected world, we gorge ourselves on endless content—mindlessly scrolling, passively consuming, and unconsciously absorbing whatever flashes across our screens. We feast on viral trends, celebrity opinions, and algorithm-driven distractions while starving our spirits of real nourishment. But true growth doesn't happen by accident. *Transformation requires intention.*

The apostle Paul operated in undeniable anointing—church planter, miracle worker, author of Scripture. Yet the Bereans refused to accept even his teachings without scrutiny. While others blindly followed or outright rejected his message, these spiritual pioneers did something radical: they engaged. Night and day, they cross-referenced Paul's words with Scripture, verifying truth for themselves (Acts 17:11).

> *I was living on spiritual fast food while starving for a personal encounter with the Living Bread.*

This wasn't skepticism—it was *wisdom in action.*

The Bereans' example matters now more than ever. We're drowning in a sea of self-proclaimed experts:

» Social media gurus peddling half-truths
» Celebrity preachers prioritizing crowds over conviction
» Podcasters repackaging opinions as revelation

Shockingly few people emulate the Bereans' discipline. We retweet before researching, share before scrutinizing, and adopt beliefs because they're trending rather than true.

When we outsource our discernment:

1) **We become spiritually malnourished**—We feed on fast-food faith instead of the meat of God's Word (Hebrews 5:14).
2) **We risk deception**—Persuasive speakers easily sweep us into error (Ephesians 4:14).
3) **We forfeit personal revelation**—We settle for secondhand faith instead of encountering Truth Himself.

The path to authentic spiritual maturity requires:

» Daily engagement with Scripture, not just reading but studying (2 Timothy 2:15).
» A discerning spirit, testing every message against God's unchanging Word (1 John 4:1).
» Courage to question even respected leaders when their words don't align with Truth.

This is your wake-up call.

In an age of information overload, spiritual survival depends on intentionality. Will you be a passive consumer or a Berean believer committed to verifying truth at all costs? The quality of your spiritual diet determines the strength of your faith. Choose wisely.

"Like newborn infants, long for the pure spiritual milk, that by it you may grow up into salvation."
—1 Peter 2:2 (ESV)

FROM SECONDHAND FAITH TO SPIRITUAL DISCERNMENT

There was a season when my spiritual diet consisted entirely of prepackaged truths—hand-me-down sermons, borrowed interpretations, and recycled revelations. Every question about God sent me scrambling to my favorite preacher's latest podcast or my mentor's well-worn commentaries. While these resources were valuable, I awoke to a sobering reality: I was living on spiritual fast food while starving for a personal encounter with the Living Bread.

The moment of transformation came unexpectedly. A popular sermon—eloquent, emotionally charged, and dripping with apparent anointing—suddenly triggered my spirit's alarm system. Instead of swallowing it whole as I once would have, I did something radical: I opened my Bible. Line by line, I compared the preacher's words with Scripture. What I discovered shocked me—glittering generalities that sparkled in the delivery but crumbled under biblical scrutiny.

That day, I became a Berean.

Just as eagles refuse to scavenge rotten carcasses but seek fresh, life-giving prey, I made three intentional shifts:

1) **Curated my teachers**—I no longer accepted every popular voice but used God's plumb line to test them all (1 John 4:1).
2) **Prioritized primary sources**—I shifted from commentary-dependence to wrestling directly with Scripture (Acts 17:11).
3) **Scheduled sacred appointments**—I protected daily time for prayer and Word engagement as non-negotiable spiritual meals.

The results were transformative:
» My prayers shifted from repetitive petitions to revelatory dialogues.
» My discernment became razor-sharp, spotting truth from error instinctively.
» My faith moved from fragile to unshakable, built on personal encounters, not secondhand testimonies.

THE BEREAN CHALLENGE FOR EVERY EAGLE BELIEVER

Ask yourself:
- » Do direct downloads from heaven or repackaged revelations from others fuel your spiritual life?
- » Do you spend more time consuming Christian content than contending for personal encounters?
- » Are you satisfied with knowing about God through teachers or desperate to know Him face-to-face?

The noble Bereans modeled the only safe path in this age of spiritual counterfeits through their:

1) **Hunger for truth**—They received Paul's message with eager anticipation.

2) **Biblical verification**—They "examined the Scriptures daily" like forensic investigators.

3) **Personal revelation**—They sought not just information but transformation.

This is your moment of emancipation from spiritual dependency. God doesn't reward laziness—He crowns seeking (Hebrews 11:6). Tear off the training wheels of perpetual spiritual infancy. The Most High waits to reveal Himself to you—not just through others but *face-to-face*. Will you settle for a borrowed faith, or storm the throne room for your own?

"When the Spirit of truth comes, he will guide you into all the truth."
—John 16:13 (ESV)

The question is—**are you willing to be led?**

With today's technology, we live in an age of unprecedented access to information. At the tap of a screen, we can explore endless opinions, ideologies, and teachings from around the world. Yet, this abundance comes at a cost: we are constantly bombarded with data, overwhelmed by noise, and pulled in countless directions. Social media feeds, news cycles, and endless streams of content compete for our attention, often leaving us more distracted than informed.

In this digital age, the challenge isn't finding information—it's filtering it. How do we discern truth from deception, wisdom from noise, and what truly matters from what merely demands our attention? Social media, news cycles, entertainment, and the people around you are all feeding you something. But the real question is: what are you consuming? And how is it shaping your life? Just because something is available does not mean it is beneficial. Many Christians blindly follow charismatic speakers without testing their words against Scripture. Some get spiritually lazy, preferring to be spoon-fed rather than actively seeking God. Others allow negative influences—doubt, fear, and toxic entertainment to corrupt their thinking. Like the Bereans, we must test everything. To do this, ask yourself the following questions:

1) Is what I am consuming bringing me closer to God or pushing me further away?
2) Am I developing personal revelation or just depending on others?
3) Am I engaging with the Word of God daily or only on Sundays?

It is not enough to hear good teaching—you need to experience God personally.

Information inspires, but revelation transforms.

A good sermon can stir you, but personal study will root you.

A pastor can encourage you, but only God can give you the wisdom that is equal to your prophetic destiny.

DEVELOPING A HEALTHY SPIRITUAL DIET

The following can help you cultivate a strong spiritual diet, and soar above the noise:

1) **Commit to daily Scripture study**—Don't just read devotionals; go deep into God's Word for yourself.
2) **Pray for understanding**—Ask the Holy Spirit to reveal deeper truths to you.
3) **Filter teachings through Scripture**—If a message doesn't align with the Bible, reject it.
4) **Be selective about what you consume**—Cut out spiritual junk food (empty distractions, misleading teachings, worldly influences).
5) **Seek God directly**—Develop a personal relationship with God, beyond just church or preachers.

Your growth is your responsibility. No one else can build your faith for you. You must take ownership of your spiritual nourishment and feed on what strengthens you. Jesus said: "Man shall not live by bread alone, but by every word that proceeds from the mouth of God" (Matthew 4:4, NKJV). Are you feeding your spirit with fresh revelation from God, or are you surviving on spiritual leftovers from others? The choice is yours—be a vulture/chicken Christian who feeds on dead words or an eagle Christian who soars with fresh revelation and strength. Your destiny depends on what you feed your mind, body, and spirit. Choose wisely.

"People tend to be generous when sharing their nonsense, fear, and ignorance. And while they seem quite eager to feed you their negativity, please remember that sometimes the diet we need to be on is a spiritual and emotional one. Be cautious

with what you feed your mind and soul. Fuel yourself with positivity and let that fuel propel you into positive action."

—Steve Maraboli[22]

FROM SCRAPS TO SOARING

The defining difference between an eagle Christian and a chicken Christian comes down to one powerful factor: appetite. What we consume—spiritually, mentally, and emotionally—determines the depth of our faith, the strength of our character, and the height of our destiny. Just as an eagle refuses to feed on anything lifeless or decayed, an eagle Christian is deliberate about what they allow into their spirit, mind, and heart. They understand that their choices today shape their spiritual flight tomorrow.

Eagle Christians are relentless in their pursuit of true nourishment. They don't settle for spiritual scraps or hollow substitutes—they crave the living Word, fresh revelation, and the kind of truth that transforms. They know that growth isn't accidental; it's intentional. They prioritize time in Scripture, not just for knowledge but for encounter. They surround themselves with voices that challenge, inspire, and align with God's purpose. And they fiercely guard their spiritual gates, ensuring that

> *If you're not growing, it's not a condemnation; it's an invitation.*

---

22 Dr. Steve Maraboli, "People tend to be generous . . . positive action," *Alabama Public Health* (Report, p. 8), 7 Sept. 2016, https://www.alabamapublichealth.gov/alphtn/assets/090716SwansonHandouts.pdf.

what they watch, listen to, and speak reflects faith, wisdom, and divine purpose.

On the other hand, chicken Christians feed on whatever is convenient. They consume surface-level teachings, chase popular opinions, and indulge in distractions that leave them spiritually malnourished. Fear, negativity, and mindless entertainment drain their faith, keeping them grounded when they were meant to soar. Without discernment, they allow anything to shape their beliefs—and wonder why they feel weak, stuck, or powerless.

But here's the turning point: Your spiritual appetite isn't fixed—it can shift. If you're not growing, it's not a condemnation; it's an invitation. Just as physical food fuels the body, your spiritual diet fuels your faith. What you consume determines whether you live in fear or boldness, stagnation or purpose. If you've been feeding on fear, you'll live in fear. If you've been consuming doubt, doubt will dominate you. But if you nourish yourself with God's Word, you will rise—strong, courageous, and unstoppable.

So, how do you shift your appetite? Start with these steps:

1) **Replace fear with faith.** Speak God's promises over your life—not the world's panic.
2) **Guard your gates.** Be ruthless about what you allow into your mind and spirit.
3) **Seek fresh revelation.** Ask God to open your eyes to deeper truths in His Word.

When you begin to feed on what truly satisfies, transformation follows. Fear loses its grip. Negativity gives way to hope. Stagnation breaks, and divine purpose takes flight.

The choice is yours. Will you keep pecking at scraps, or will you feast on what empowers you to soar? The journey starts now—one decision, one thought, one intentional step at a time. Rise up. Your eagle destiny awaits.

GUARDING THE GATES AND RISING ABOVE A CHICKEN MENTALITY

> *And he looked, and, behold, there was a cake baken on the coals, and a cruse of water at his head. And he did eat and drink, and laid him down again.*
>
> *And the angel of the LORD came again the second time, and touched him, and said, Arise and eat; because the journey is too great for thee.*
>
> *And he arose, and did eat and drink, and went in the strength of that meat forty days and forty nights unto Horeb the mount of God.* —1 Kings 19:6-8 (KJV)

This powerful scripture became a wake-up call for me—a divine revelation that what I feed on determines the strength of my journey. Imagine setting out on a grueling expedition with no fuel, no preparation, and no energy. You wouldn't last long. The same is true for your spiritual walk. When Elijah was exhausted, God didn't just tell him to rest—He commanded him to eat. That single meal sustained him for forty days and nights. Why? Because your spiritual diet determines your endurance, your resilience, and ultimately, your destiny.

There was a season in my life when I was going through the motions—praying half-heartedly, skimming Scripture, and passively listening to sermons. But when trials hit, I crumbled. My faith wavered. My peace evaporated. I was running on fumes, and it showed. Then, one day, the Holy Spirit pierced my heart with this truth: *You cannot complete the assignment I've given you if you keep feeding on what doesn't nourish your spirit.*

That was my turning point. I made a decision: No more spiritual junk food. No more half-hearted devotion. I began to feast on God's Word—not just reading it but digging deep, meditating, and letting it transform me. I replaced sporadic prayers with a disciplined prayer life. I stopped letting fear and negativity dominate my thoughts and instead renewed my mind with truth, and something incredible happened—my strength returned. When new challenges arose, I didn't collapse in fear. I stood firm. Why? Because I was no longer running on empty—I was fueled by revelation.

> *I realized that you don't rise to the level of your goals; you rise to the level of your nourishment.*

Proverbs 4:23 warns, "guard your heart, for everything you do flows from it." In today's world, distractions are relentless. Information floods in from every direction, and if we're not careful, we'll consume things that weaken rather than strengthen us. I had to take radical action to protect my spiritual gates—my eyes, ears, and mouth—because what enters them shapes my entire life.

1) **The Eye Gate (what I watch):** I used to mindlessly scroll through social media, binge-watch empty entertainment, and expose myself to content that left me drained. But I realized that what I watch shapes what I think—and what I think shapes who I become.

My shift: I unfollowed negativity, comparison traps, and fear-driven content. I replaced passive scrolling with intentional viewing—sermons, uplifting books, and wisdom-filled teachings. I set boundaries on entertainment, asking, "Does this feed my spirit or drain it?"

2) **The Ear Gate (what I listen to):** I used to let my ears absorb anything—gossip, toxic conversations, news cycles designed to incite fear, and even music that didn't align with my faith. Over time, I noticed how these sounds were rewiring my mindset.

My shift: I curated my auditory environment—worship music, faith-building podcasts, and Scripture-filled meditations. I started my mornings with truth (devotionals, declarations, or sermons) to set the tone for the day. I became selective in conversations, choosing to engage in what edified rather than eroded my spirit.

3) **The Mouth Gate (what I speak):** I had to confront a hard truth: my words were betraying my faith. I spoke doubt more than declarations, worry more than worship, and complaints more than confidence. But Luke 6:45 says, "Out of the abundance of the heart, the mouth speaks." If my words were weak, it was because my spiritual diet was lacking.

My shift: I replaced fear-filled words with faith-filled decrees—speaking God's promises over my life. I paused before speaking, asking, "Do these words align with victory or defeat?" I used my voice to build up, not tear down—myself and others.

When I took control of my spiritual diet and guarded my gates, everything changed. Fear lost its grip. Anxiety faded. My faith grew stronger, sharper, and unshakable. I realized that you don't rise to the level of your goals; you rise to the level of your nourishment.

If you've been feeling spiritually weak, stuck, or overwhelmed, ask yourself: What have I been feeding my spirit? What am I allowing through my gates? Do my words reflect faith or fear?

The journey to rising above a "chicken mentality" starts with one intentional choice at a time. Guard your gates. Feed your spirit. And watch how God fuels you for the road ahead—further, stronger, and higher than you ever imagined. The call is clear: eat right. Your destiny depends on it.

> *Yesterday's revelation won't sustain you in today's battles.*

THE SIGN OF SPIRITUAL HEALTH

An eagle that stops hunting loses its strength—and, eventually, its life. It must keep seeking fresh prey to maintain its power, speed, and dominance in the skies. The same is true for you. If you are truly alive in Christ, you should have a relentless hunger for God's Word and His presence. A dull or absent spiritual appetite isn't just a minor issue—it's a warning sign of declining spiritual health.

Many believers make the fatal mistake of living off past encounters with God. They reminisce about the miracles of yesterday but have no fresh fire, no new testimonies, no present-tense breakthroughs. But here's the truth: yesterday's revelation won't sustain you in today's battles. God is the I AM—not the I WAS. He wants you to seek Him daily, hear His voice daily, and experience His power daily. Don't settle for stale bread—demand fresh manna. Stop clinging to old manna. The Israelites couldn't survive on yesterday's provision—and neither can you (Exodus 16:20). Stop living on past victories. If your last testimony is from five years ago, your faith is starving. Stop being satisfied with surface-level knowledge. God invites you deeper—into fresh revelation, greater intimacy, and unexplored dimensions of His glory.

Jesus didn't teach us to pray, "Give us yesterday's bread." He said, "Give us this day our daily bread" (Matthew 6:11). Why? Because life with God is a daily pursuit. You can't sprint a marathon on last week's meals. Elijah needed supernatural nourishment for his journey—and so do you (1 Kings 19:6-8).

Just as physical hunger signals your body's need for nourishment, spiritual hunger is the evidence of a healthy, thriving faith. If you feel distant from God, don't just ask, "Why isn't God speaking?" Ask yourself: Am I even hungry for Him?

If you feed on fear, you'll live in bondage.

If you feed on distractions, you'll grow spiritually weak.

But if you feast on God's Word, you'll develop unshakable faith, divine endurance, and the strength to conquer every battle.

God is offering you fresh bread—through His Word, through prayer, and through worship. The question is: will you eat, or will you let your spirit starve?

WHERE HUNGER MEETS PREPARATION

Soaring doesn't happen overnight. Before an eagle rules the skies, it endures a season of *training, testing,* and *transformation*—often in the wilderness. This isn't punishment; it's *preparation*. The wilderness is where God:

» **Prunes** what's unnecessary.
» **Strengthens** what's weak.
» **Prepares** you for greater things.

In the next chapter, we'll dive into how this season—though challenging—is your divine setup for elevation. The hunger you feel? It's not a sign of abandonment. It's the prelude to your breakthrough.

It's time to reflect: feast or famine? Audit your spiritual diet. Are you feeding on life-giving truth or spiritual junk food? Seek God like your life depends on it—because it does. Embrace the wilderness. It's not your burial ground—it's your launching pad.

The journey ahead demands more than yesterday's faith. It's time to eat, grow, and rise. Your training ground awaits. Let's begin.

> An eagle's wings are only as strong
> as what it consumes.
> You cannot feast on fear and expect to soar in faith.
> Every thought, every word, every truth you ingest—
> this is the holy diet that determines your altitude.
> —Tessy Tanyi

CHAPTER 15

THE WILDERNESS EXPERIENCE

Your Training Ground for Greatness

The journey to greatness is never a straight road. Just as an eagle must endure a season of discomfort before it fully learns to soar, so must we go through our own wilderness experience—a period of testing, transformation, and preparation for our destiny. Imagine a young eagle nurtured in the comfort of its nest. It has grown under the protective wings of its mother, never knowing hardship. But there comes a time when the mother eagle forces the eaglet out of the nest—not to harm it but to teach it to fly. The once-comfortable home becomes unfamiliar as soft feathers and warm linings are removed, exposing sharp thorns. The eaglet, confused and frightened, can no longer rest where it once felt secure. The mother stops feeding it directly, compelling the young eagle to fend for itself. And then, the most terrifying moment arrives—the mother eagle pushes it off the cliff. To the eaglet, this feels like betrayal. Why would the one who once cared for it now seem to abandon it? But in reality, this is a necessary process—for it is in that freefall that the eaglet discovers its wings. It struggles at first, flapping desperately, but then it begins to catch the wind, to rise, and, finally, to soar.

Like the eaglet, every eagle Christian must go through a wilderness experience. It is the phase where God removes the safety nets, forces you out of your comfort zone, and teaches you to rely on Him alone. It is the season of training, where your character is refined, your endurance tested, and your faith stretched to new heights. The wilderness is not a punishment—it is God's classroom. Just as every great leader in the Bible—Moses, Joseph, Elijah, David, and even Jesus—had to pass through their own wilderness before stepping into their destiny, you, too must walk through this refining season. It may feel lonely, uncertain, and even painful, but it is the only way to soar.

This chapter will prepare you for the wilderness experience. It will help you understand why it is necessary, what to expect, and how to emerge from it stronger and ready to fulfill your divine purpose. Just like the eaglet, your time in the wilderness is not the end—it is the beginning of your flight.

UNDERSTANDING THE WILDERNESS

The wilderness experience is often misunderstood. Many assume it is a punishment or a consequence of wrong decisions, but in reality, it is a divine setup for elevation. It is a place of isolation, where the distractions of comfort, familiarity, and people-pleasing are stripped away. It is a place where God takes you aside to work on you, shape you, and transform you before He releases you into the fullness of your calling. The wilderness is the space between your past and your destiny. It is the season of separation from your old ways, old habits, and even old relationships so that you can step fully into your new identity as an eagle Christian. This transition can feel uncomfortable, slow, and lonely. But just like the mother eagle removes the soft lining from the nest to push her eaglets to fly, God allows certain challenges, tests, and pruning seasons to prepare us for our next level.

The wilderness experience is a common theme throughout the Bible, often symbolizing a period of testing, transformation, and preparation for greater assignments. If God allowed His people to pass through it, why should you expect to avoid it? Below are some key biblical figures who went through wilderness experiences:

1) Moses (forty years in the wilderness—Exodus 3:1)

Experience: After killing an Egyptian, Moses fled to the wilderness of Midian, where he spent forty years as a shepherd before encountering God in the burning bush. Later, he led the Israelites through the wilderness for another forty years.

Purpose: Preparation for leadership, humility, and learning to trust God.

Lesson: Sometimes, separation is necessary before elevation.

2) The Israelites (forty years in the wilderness—Exodus 16:35)

Experience: After their deliverance from Egypt, the Israelites wandered in the desert for forty years due to their disobedience and lack of faith.

Purpose: To test their faith, obedience, and dependence on God.

Lesson: Delayed promises are often the result of disobedience and lack of trust in God.

3) Elijah (forty days in the wilderness—1 Kings 19:4-8)
   Experience: After confronting King Ahab and Queen Jezebel, Elijah fled to the wilderness in fear and exhaustion, where an angel sustained him and where he later encountered God in a still small voice.
   Purpose: Renewal, spiritual strength, and guidance for his next assignment.
   Lesson: God provides and speaks even in moments of despair.
4) David (years of hiding in the wilderness—1 Samuel 23:14)
   Experience: Before becoming king, David spent years hiding in the wilderness as King Saul sought to kill him.
   Purpose: To develop leadership, patience, and trust in God's timing.
   Lesson: God's promises require preparation before fulfillment.
5) Job (wilderness of suffering—Job 1-42)
   Experience: Job lost everything—his wealth, health, and family. His season of suffering felt like a wilderness.
   Purpose: To test his faith and refine his understanding of God's sovereignty.
   Lesson: Suffering refines faith and leads to a deeper relationship with God.
6) John the Baptist (life in the wilderness—Luke 1:80)
   Experience: John lived in the wilderness, preparing the way for Christ through preaching and fasting.
   Purpose: To develop boldness and a prophetic voice.
   Lesson: Separation leads to divine revelation and purpose.
7) Jesus (forty days in the wilderness—Matthew 4:1-11)
   Experience: Before beginning His public ministry, Jesus fasted and Satan tempted Him in the wilderness.

Purpose: To be tested and prepared for His mission.

Lesson: Spiritual battles precede great assignments.

8) Paul (three years in the Arabian wilderness—Galatians 1:17-18).

   Experience: After his dramatic conversion on the road to Damascus, Paul didn't immediately step into public ministry. Instead, he withdrew to the wilderness of Arabia for an estimated three years. During this time, he was separated from the apostles and the spotlight—hidden, yet being deeply formed.

   Purpose: Revelation, transformation, and reorientation. God stripped away Saul's old identity and rebuilt Paul's new one in Christ.

   Lesson: Before God uses you publicly, He often shapes you privately. Silence is not absence—it's preparation.

9) Hagar (wilderness of Beersheba—Genesis 21:14-19)

   Experience: After being mistreated by Sarai, Hagar fled into the wilderness—pregnant, alone, and without a plan. There, by a spring in the desert, the Angel of the Lord met her, called her by name, and gave her both comfort and purpose.

   Purpose: To encounter God personally and discover her identity beyond rejection. Hagar became the first person in Scripture to give God a name: El Roi, "the God who sees me."

   Lesson: God sees and provides for the abandoned.

10) Jonah (wilderness of the deep—Jonah 1-2)

    Experience: After running from God's assignment, Jonah found himself swallowed by a great fish and submerged in the depths of the sea for three days and nights. In the darkness, with no escape route, he finally surrendered and cried out to God.

Purpose: Correction, surrender, and redirection. The isolation forced Jonah to confront his disobedience and realign with God's will.

Lesson: You can't outrun God's calling. Sometimes, the wilderness isn't about where you go—it's about what God is doing to bring your heart back into alignment with His.

11) Jacob (wilderness at Bethel and Peniel—Genesis 28:10–22; 32:22–31)

Experience: Jacob fled into the wilderness after deceiving his father and stealing Esau's blessing. Alone at Bethel, he encountered God in a dream. Years later, at Peniel, he wrestled through the night with an angel of the Lord—fighting for a blessing and walking away changed.

Purpose: Identity transformation, divine encounter, and heart refinement. Jacob entered the wilderness as a deceiver and emerged as Israel—the one who wrestles with God and prevails.

Lesson: Sometimes, God has to isolate us to confront what's in us. The wilderness isn't just where we run—it's where we *wrestle* and where God renames us for what's ahead.

12) Joseph (wilderness of Egypt—Genesis 37–41)

Experience: Betrayed by his brothers, sold into slavery, falsely accused, and imprisoned—Joseph's wilderness didn't look like sand and stone but like chains and silence. For over a decade, he lived in a land of affliction far from the dreams God had given him.

Purpose: Character development, leadership training, and divine positioning. God used Egypt to refine Joseph, elevate him, and prepare him to save nations.

Lesson: The wilderness can feel like a detour, but it's often the direct path to destiny. What others meant for evil, God can use for good—if you stay faithful in the unseen.

APOSTLE PAUL'S THREE-YEAR WILDERNESS EXPERIENCE

Before the apostle Paul became one of the most influential figures in Christianity, he went through a crucial wilderness experience—a season of separation, deep spiritual transformation, and preparation for his mission. Paul, formerly known as Saul, needed a wilderness experience. He was a devout Pharisee who zealously persecuted Christians. He was well-versed in Jewish law but spiritually blind to the truth of Christ. After his dramatic conversion on the road to Damascus, Paul did not immediately begin preaching to the masses or step into ministry leadership. Instead, he withdrew into the wilderness of Arabia for three years, where the Holy Spirit personally taught and equipped him for the great calling ahead.

Paul briefly mentions this period in Galatians 1:15-18:

But when God, who set me apart from my mother's womb and called me by his grace, was pleased to reveal his Son in me so that I might preach him among the Gentiles, my immediate response was not to consult any human being. I did not go up to Jerusalem to see those who were apostles before I was, but I went into Arabia. Later I returned to Damascus. Then, after three years, I went up to Jerusalem to get acquainted with Cephas and stayed with him fifteen days.

This passage reveals a few key things:

1) **He did not seek human approval.** After his encounter with Christ, Paul did not immediately go to the other apostles for

guidance. Instead, he chose solitude with God, allowing the Holy Spirit to shape his understanding of the gospel.

2) **He went to Arabia.** This was likely a time of prayer, fasting, and direct revelation from God. Paul needed to unlearn his former Pharisaic mindset and fully embrace the message of grace.

3) **He spent three years in preparation.** Just as Jesus spent forty days in the wilderness before beginning His ministry, and Moses spent forty years in the desert before leading Israel, Paul's three years in Arabia were a necessary period of spiritual refinement before his global mission.

Paul's wilderness season was a period of:

- » **Spiritual detox:** Letting go of legalism and embracing grace.
- » **Divine training:** Receiving direct revelation from Jesus as he later affirmed in Galatians 1:11-12, "I did not receive it from any man, nor was I taught it; rather, I received it by revelation from Jesus Christ."
- » **Personal transformation:** Becoming the man who would later say, "For to me, to live is Christ and to die is gain" (Philippians 1:21).

Like Paul, an eagle Christian must go through a wilderness experience before soaring. Eagles do not stay grounded with chickens—they retreat to high places to renew their strength. Paul's time in Arabia mirrors this as he withdrew to be alone with God before taking flight in ministry. His time of isolation was not punishment but preparation for the great mission ahead.

This teaches us an important lesson:

» Before God entrusts you with a divine assignment, He will often lead you into a season of preparation, separation, and refinement.
» True revelation and strength come from time spent alone with God, away from distractions.
» Your wilderness is not a delay—it is your training ground.
» Paul emerged from Arabia empowered and unshakable in his calling. He went on to write nearly two-thirds of the New Testament and spread the gospel to the Gentiles, transforming the course of history.

Here are the key takeaways from the biblical wilderness experience:
1) Wilderness is a place of preparation.
2) Trials refine and strengthen faith.
3) God never leaves His people in the wilderness forever.
4) Every great leader went through a wilderness before stepping into their calling.

So, if you find yourself in a wilderness season, take heart—God is preparing you for something greater. Stay rooted in Him, and when the time comes, you will rise and soar like an eagle, just as Paul did.

MY PERSONAL WILDERNESS EXPERIENCE

I once believed that declaring my commitment to follow God wholeheartedly would be met with celebration—that people would cheer me on, roll out the red carpet, and welcome me into the journey of faith with open arms. But my wilderness experience taught me otherwise. Instead of support, I encountered opposition—not from strangers but from those closest to me. Rather than laying out a red carpet, they pulled away even the small rug I was standing on. I quickly realized that the enemy often works through the people around us, creating obstacles and resistance to discourage us from pursuing God's calling.

My own wilderness journey began the moment I decided to pursue God's calling on my life. Before then, I was like an eaglet safe in the nest—comfortable, unaware of what lay beyond, and not yet ready to fly. But when God began to stir my heart and awaken me to my divine assignment, everything around me shifted. At first, I thought stepping into my calling would be met with celebration, encouragement, and support from those around me. But instead of applause, I was met with resistance. People I once looked up to—mentors, friends, even some in the faith—began to question my calling.

> *If you never face resistance, your calling is not a threat to the enemy.*

"God can't use you."
"You don't have what it takes."
"You're not qualified."
"You don't fit the mold of someone God would use."

These words cut deep. I was misjudged, rejected, and ridiculed. Some even suggested that I was being arrogant for thinking that God could use me in any significant way. I was told to stay in my lane, to not get ahead of myself, and that if I truly loved God, I should just settle into the background and serve quietly. I remember crying out to God, asking, "Lord, did I hear You wrong? Why does following Your call feel like I am losing everything? Why am I facing so much opposition?" I felt isolated, misunderstood, and, at times, even doubted myself. But then, God reminded me of the eagle. Just as the mother eagle removes the comforts of the nest, so the eaglet can learn to fly, God was allowing my rejection to propel me forward. The very people who pushed me away were unknowingly pushing me into His presence, into deeper prayer, and into greater reliance on His voice instead of human validation.

In my wilderness, God stripped away every crutch I had been leaning on. He showed me that it was never about my qualifications but His calling. It was never about my ability but His power. He reminded me of how He used Moses—a stuttering, insecure man—to lead a nation, how He chose David—a shepherd boy—to become king, and how He called Gideon—a man hiding in fear—to be a mighty warrior. Through this process, I learned a powerful truth: opposition is confirmation. If you never face resistance, your calling is not a threat to the enemy. But the moment you step into the fullness of who God has called you to be, the attacks will come. People will misunderstand you. They will question your motives. They will try to discourage you.

But hold on.

> The people who make the biggest impact are those who have learned to stand alone with God before standing in front of crowds.

Just like Joseph, who was thrown into a pit before he reached the palace. . . .

Just like Moses, who spent years in the wilderness before leading the Israelites. . . .

Just like David, who was hunted before he took the throne. . . .

Just like Jesus, who was tested in the wilderness before launching His ministry. . . .

Looking back, I now thank God for my wilderness. The rejection I faced was the redirection I needed. The loneliness pushed me into deeper intimacy with Him. The doubts forced me to seek His truth for myself. The pain built a strength in me that I never knew I needed. So, if you find yourself in the wilderness right now, do not fear. Do not retreat. It is not the end—it is just the beginning. You are not being buried; you are being planted. Stay the course, trust God, and know that when this season is over, you will not just fly—you will soar.

Even in the wilderness, God was in control. He knew where I was, He saw me, He was with me, and He was preparing me for something greater. I made up my mind to not resist the process. Instead, I embraced it, knowing that the wilderness is not my final destination—it is the pathway to the fulfillment of my destiny.

One of the hardest parts of my wilderness experience was loneliness. I lost friends. I lost comfort. I lost the familiar. But I found God in a way I never had before. This is where most people give up. They go back to what is familiar because the loneliness is too much. But let me tell you this: loneliness is not abandonment—it is preparation. Jesus often withdrew to be alone with God. If you cannot handle being alone, you are not ready for leadership. The people who make the biggest impact are those who have learned to stand alone with God before standing in front of crowds. If you are too afraid of losing people, you will lose your purpose instead. Choose wisely. Moreover, the Lord used my wilderness season to remind me that He doesn't call crowds. He calls individuals, and as the individual follows Him, He empowers that individual to draw crowds to Him. He also taught me that one with Him is a majority, so in reality, even though it felt lonely, I was never alone.

There were four major things that happened in my wilderness experience:

1) **Discomfort set in.** Just as the eaglet suddenly finds its nest uncomfortable, I started feeling uneasy in places I once enjoyed. What used to excite me no longer satisfied me. I began to feel an inner longing for something more. This was a sign that God was preparing me to leave my old environment.
2) **Separation began.** I found myself naturally withdrawing from certain relationships, activities, or habits that no longer aligned with God's purpose for my life.
3) **The waiting period began.** This is the most challenging part. You know that you are not where you used to be, but you also know you are not yet where you need to be. It feels like time is standing still, but in reality, God is working behind the scenes.
4) **I was misunderstood.** The very people who once supported me began to question my decisions. They claimed I was "different" or that I had changed, and the truth is, they were right—I had changed. But what they saw as a problem was actually growth, a necessary transformation on my journey to fulfill God's calling.

God's voice was clear to me: *You must endure the wilderness before you can walk in your purpose. This season is not meant to destroy you—it is meant to develop you.* And God was right—it did develop me! Here are some ways that it changed me, and I strongly believe it will do the same for you:

1) **It will remove your chicken mentality:** You will dissociate yourself from pigeons and chickens—those who live in mediocrity and settle for less. But before you can fully function as an eagle, God has to remove every lingering mentality of fear, doubt, and complacency. This is your spiritual surgery—the process of removing everything that hinders your ability to soar.

2) **It will prune you for your next level:** Just as trees are pruned to bear more fruit, you must be pruned of unhealthy attachments, wrong mindsets, and distractions. If you are carrying too much baggage, you cannot fly.

3) **It will strengthen your relationship with God:** In the wilderness, you will learn to depend solely on God. This is the time to fast, pray, and study the Word like never before. God will draw you closer to Him so that as you begin to soar, you will always remain connected to your source.

Here's how to navigate this season with purpose and resilience:

1) **Stay focused on your purpose:** Keep your eyes fixed on your calling, not on the distractions around you. The wilderness can feel overwhelming, but a clear vision will keep you anchored and moving forward.

2) **Guard your heart and mind:** Don't let negativity, doubts, or the opinions of others shake your faith. Protect your heart by filling it with God's promises and truth.

3) **Strengthen your relationship with God:** Let prayer, fasting, and studying Scripture become a natural part of your life. The

wilderness is a season to draw closer to God and hear His voice with greater clarity.

4) **Be patient, but keep moving:** Your breakthrough may take time, but don't give up. Even when progress feels slow, keep taking steps of faith and trust that God is working behind the scenes.

5) **Surround yourself with the right people:** Align yourself with spiritual mentors, wise leaders, and faith-filled believers who can guide, encourage, and challenge you along the journey.

6) **Resist the urge to complain:** Rather than viewing the wilderness as a burden, see it as a season of preparation. Shift your perspective and embrace the lessons it brings.

7) **Be faithful in the small things:** Before Moses led a nation, he was faithful as a shepherd. Be diligent and obedient in every task God gives you, no matter how small it may seem.

8) **Hold tight to God's promises:** Just as Moses never lost sight of God's promise to Israel, hold firmly to His Word even in difficult seasons. His promises will sustain and guide you.

9) **Trust God's timing:** Don't try to force your way out of the wilderness. Surrender to God's process, knowing that His timing is always perfect. What seems like a delay is actually divine preparation.

10) **Believe that this season will end:** The wilderness is not your final destination. God is leading you into something greater. Stay hopeful, stay faithful, and trust that He is preparing you for what's next.

As we conclude this chapter, take a moment to reflect on the significance of nourishing your spirit and mind. Just as an eagle carefully chooses its food, never settling for anything lifeless or decayed, you must be intentional about what you consume spiritually and mentally. You have learned the importance of guarding your gates, seeking fresh revelation, and feeding on God's Word—the ultimate source of strength and truth.

Always remember this: your spiritual appetite determines your altitude. If you constantly feed on fear, negativity, and doubt, you will find yourself stuck—grounded in uncertainty, unable to rise above limitations. But when you nourish yourself with God's promises and truth, you develop the strength to soar beyond obstacles and claim the heights He has prepared for you.

However, soaring doesn't happen overnight. Before an eagle masters the skies, it endures a season of preparation—a period of testing, training, and transformation. This crucial time is often marked by the wilderness—a place of uncertainty, challenge, and solitude. Though it may feel like isolation, the wilderness is where strength is forged, faith is refined, and true greatness is developed.

BUILDING RESILIENCE

> *"Yet because this widow keeps bothering me, I will see that she gets justice, so that she won't eventually come and attack me!"*
> —Luke 18:5

In the next chapter, we will explore the divine moment when private preparation meets public purpose. After the wilderness comes the unveiling—not just of what you've endured but of who you've become. It will further reveal how God often does His greatest refining in the dark, away from applause, recognition, or clarity.

*The wilderness isn't God's abandonment—
it's His advanced training course.
No eagle learns to soar in a cage.
These barren places?
They're your runway.*
—Tessy Tanyi

CHAPTER 16

FROM HIDDEN TO HERALDED

*How God Reveals What
He Refined in Secret*

You've survived the silence. The season when you felt unseen, unnoticed, and maybe even unnecessary. The place where you prayed without answers, served without recognition, and grew without applause.

What if that hiddenness wasn't punishment—but preparation?

As we read earlier, throughout Scripture, God has a pattern: before He reveals, He refines. Before He puts someone on display, He takes them through the shadows. Moses was hidden in the desert, David in the fields, Joseph in a prison, and even Jesus in obscurity for thirty years.

The wilderness trained your spirit. Now, this next season will require your obedience, your readiness, and your character.

You weren't being forgotten.

You were being forged.

And now, when the time is right, God doesn't just bring you out—He brings you forth.

From hidden to heralded. From preparation to purpose.

Just as Joseph rose from prison to palace, David from shepherd to king, and Esther from orphan to queen, God specializes in taking those He's hidden—and revealing them at the appointed time. You were never overlooked—you were being overprepared.

This chapter will emphasize:
- » The value of hidden seasons and why God conceals before He reveals.
- » How to recognize when your "set time" has come (Psalm 102:13).
- » The importance of character over platform—why who you are matters more than where you're seen.
- » Encouragement not to rush the process or promote yourself prematurely.
- » How to walk in humility and boldness when God opens the door for visibility and influence.

You'll be reminded that God hasn't forgotten you. What felt like obscurity was divine incubation. When He says the time is right, what was hidden will be heralded—not for your glory but for His purpose through you.

"Yet because this widow keeps bothering me, I will see that she gets justice, so that she won't eventually come and attack me!"
—Luke 18:5

In the last chapter, we walked through the wilderness—the hidden place where God forms His greatest vessels. But the wilderness is not the end of the story. The question now is this: what happens after the hiding? How do you transition from surviving in the shadows to standing in the light? The answer is resilience. Every eagle must go through pressure before it soars. The hunger you feel in your hidden season isn't a sign of abandonment—it's the prelude to your unveiling. Resilience is what determines whether you will remain buried or rise when the moment of revealing comes.

I remember sitting by the fireplace one quiet evening, watching the flames dance across the logs, and this thought dropped into my spirit: *Why do the same storms break some and build others?* Why do some rise from adversity stronger, while others stay stuck in pain? The answer came in one word: resilience.

The *Cambridge Dictionary* defines resilience as "the ability to be happy and successful again after something difficult or bad has happened." It's also "the ability of a substance to return to its usual shape after being bent, stretched, or pressed."[23] But biblically? Resilience is the grit of the gospel in motion. It's the fire God forges in the furnace of obscurity, so you're strong enough to carry what He's about to entrust to you.

Even research affirms what the Spirit reveals. Maurice Vanderpol, former president of the Boston Psychoanalytic Society, discovered that Holocaust survivors possessed something called a "plastic

> *Jesus revealed a kingdom principle: those who endure in the secret place will be rewarded in the open.*

---

23 Cambridge Dictionary Online, s.v. "resilience," https://dictionary.cambridge.org/dictionary/english/resilience.

shield"—an inner space that allowed them to reframe pain, find humor, and hold on.[24] That shield wasn't natural—it was cultivated. And so is yours.

In Luke 18:1–5, Jesus introduces us to a woman who embodied this: the persistent widow. She wasn't famous, favored, or influential—but she was *resilient*. Her persistence became her platform. Her refusal to give up became the key to her breakthrough. And in the process, Jesus revealed a kingdom principle: those who endure in the secret place will be rewarded in the open.

Resilience is the bridge between being *refined in secret* and *revealed in purpose*. It's not just about enduring trials—it's about emerging from them shaped, strengthened, and seen by God. Passion is what fuels this resilience. When your desire to obey God outweighs your fear of failing, you:

> *Vision isn't just a motivational concept—it's the compass that keeps you grounded when you're walking through the wilderness.*

» Push through every obstacle.
» Endure every hardship.
» Refuse to settle until purpose is fulfilled.

The heroes we admire weren't the smartest, strongest, or most privileged—they were simply the ones who *refused to quit in the*

---

24 Maurice Vanderpol, "Resilience: A Missing Link in Our Understanding of Survival," *Harvard Review Psychiatry* 10, no. 5 (2009): 302-306, https://doi.org/10.1080/10673220216282.

dark, so God revealed them in the light. As Dean Becker of Adaptiv Learning Systems said, "More than education, more than experience, more than training, a person's level of resilience will determine who succeeds and who fails."[25]

Your background, credentials, or circumstances don't determine whether you'll be seen. Your capacity to endure, to stretch without breaking, to stay planted while hidden does. Take the bamboo tree. It bends with the wind but never breaks. It's flexible, yet deeply rooted. You can't rush its growth—but when its season comes, it rises faster than almost anything else around it. That's you. You've been hidden, stretched, overlooked, and pressed. But you haven't broken. And now? Now, comes the *revealing*.

God never refines you for nothing. If He's allowed pressure, it's because purpose is on the other side. You were never buried. You were planted. And what He planted in secret, He is about to *herald in glory*. However, knowing you're planted isn't enough—you have to stay rooted. And the only thing that will keep you grounded, focused, and moving forward through the wilderness is vision.

VISION: THE FUEL TO FINISH YOUR WILDERNESS SEASON

At the beginning of this journey, you were asked a pivotal question: **do you have a clear vision for your life?** And if your answer was yes—*will you keep soaring when the winds grow strong?*

That question matters more than ever here. Because vision isn't just a motivational concept—it's the compass that keeps you grounded when you're walking through the wilderness.

---

25 Dean Becker, cited in Diane Coutu, "How Resilience Works, *Harvard Business Review*, May 2002, https://hbr.org/2002/05/how-resilience-works.

The wilderness is not easy. It's dry. It's quiet. It's humbling. It tests your identity and stretches your faith. And without a clear vision—**a God-given picture of where you're going and who you're becoming**—you're more likely to quit halfway, mistaking your delay for denial and your formation for failure.

Vision is what empowers you to press on when everything in you wants to pull back.

It keeps you anchored in *why* you started, even when the "how" feels uncertain.

It reminds you that **there's glory on the other side of the grit**.

Eagle Christians don't just survive the wilderness—they soar through it. But they don't soar aimlessly. Like the eagle locking its eyes on the target even through storms, you must fix your heart on what God showed you. **Vision gives the wilderness meaning.** It transforms pain into purpose and turns waiting into preparation.

When you've truly caught a glimpse of what God wants to do through your life, you don't just *hope* for change—you *push through* for it. That vision becomes a holy obsession. It demands your time, your faith, and your surrender. It becomes the fuel that makes quitting no longer an option.

Yes, there will be setbacks.

Yes, there will be seasons of silence.

But if your vision is rooted in God, then every detour is still taking you in the right direction.

So, don't lay down your vision when the road gets hard—**that's exactly when you need to hold it tighter**. Let it guide your decisions. Let it guard your focus. Let it remind you that this wilderness season is not the end—it's the middle. And if you keep moving, *glory is just ahead.*

FAILURE: THE HIGHWAY TO SUCCESS

Before God brings you forward, He often takes you through. And one of His most faithful refining tools is failure. History is filled with stories of those who were hidden in hardship before they were heralded in purpose. These weren't perfect people—they were persistent ones. They failed, fell, and faced resistance—but they refused to stay down. One of the most inspiring examples is Abraham Lincoln. He lost elections. He faced depression. He endured deep personal and professional setbacks. At any point, he could've quit, walked away, and allowed failure to define him. Instead, he let failure refine him. And because of that resilience, he didn't just succeed—he shifted history.

The road to destiny isn't lined with ease. It's shaped by struggle, paved with pressure, and refined by resistance. But that process is not punishment—it's preparation. The very burden you want to escape might be the one God is using to build you into the person He's about to reveal. That delay? That detour? That failure? It's not the end of your story—it's the hidden chapter where God is doing His deepest work. Life isn't just about arriving—it's about becoming. Every setback, every closed door, and every painful misstep is a chance to develop the character your future assignment will require. If you keep rising, keep learning, and

> *The very cross you carry in silence is preparing you for the crown God will place on you in due time.*

keep trusting the One who called you, your resilience will become the runway God uses to lift you into purpose.

So, when life bends you, don't break.

When failure visits, don't retreat—reframe.

You are not being disqualified—you are being qualified in secret.

Because when the refining is complete . . . God will bring you from hidden to heralded.

YOUR CROWN IS ENCAPSULATED IN YOUR CROSS

Jesus didn't sugarcoat the journey—He made it clear that following Him comes with a cost: *"Whoever wants to be my disciple must deny themselves and take up their cross daily and follow me"* (Luke 9:23, NIV).

That cross represents more than pain—it represents preparation. To carry your cross is to embrace the refining process God uses to shape your purpose in secret. It means walking through seasons of obscurity, responsibility, pressure, and even isolation. But here's the divine irony: the very cross you carry in silence is preparing you for the crown God will place on you in due time.

Every hero you admire—every pioneer, trailblazer, leader, or warrior—has felt the weight of their own cross. Each has wrestled with the temptation to quit. The difference between those who remained ordinary and those who stepped into their calling wasn't perfection or privilege—it was *resilience under pressure and faithfulness in the hidden place.*

There will be moments when your calling feels too heavy. Moments when you feel disqualified, unseen, or utterly exhausted, but don't despise the weight. Your crown is not apart from your cross—it's wrapped within it.

The burden you want to escape may be the very thing God is using to build you. The silence you feel? That's not neglect—it's refinement. The trials you face? They're not disqualifying you—they're qualifying you for the unveiling. Success in the kingdom doesn't belong to the strongest or most connected. It belongs to those who stay faithful through the fire, *trusting that the crown comes after the crushing.*

"But they that wait upon the LORD shall renew their *strength; they shall mount up with wings as eagles; they shall run, and not be weary;* and *they shall walk, and not faint."*
—Isaiah 40:31 (KJV)

Even the strongest get weary. The most anointed feel worn. But those who wait on the Lord—who lean in, not give up—will find a supernatural strength rising from within. Waiting isn't weakness. It's trust. It's the posture of those who know that God reveals in glory what He refines in the shadows.

Like the eagle, you weren't designed to flap harder—you were designed to rise higher. And when the weight of the cross feels unbearable, let it remind you: you're being shaped for something eternal. So, don't drop the cross. Don't give up now. Your moment of soaring is closer than you think.

WHAT NOW? THRIVING AFTER THE WILDERNESS

You've endured the hidden place.

You've been refined.

And now, you sense it—God is shifting you.

The season of silence is giving way to visibility.

But what do you do with that?

What does it look like to partner with God now that you're coming out of the wilderness?

Here are a few keys to help you not just emerge but thrive:

1) **Acknowledge the Shift.** First, recognize when your season has changed. The wilderness often dulls your hope, so it takes intentional awareness to realize: *God is moving me forward.*

   Ask yourself:
   > Has the fog started to lift?
   > Do I feel clarity where there was once confusion?
   > Is God opening doors I used to only pray about?
   > Is there a new peace about stepping out?

   Don't wait to feel "ready." If God says move, trust that He's made you ready.

2) **Stay Prayerfully Aligned.** You're not leaving the wilderness alone—you're walking out with God. This isn't the time to "move on" from intimacy but to deepen it. Let prayer shift from survival cries to *strategy conversations*. In the wilderness, prayer was survival. Prayer often sounds like, "Lord, get me through this." Now, it's strategy and surrender. After the wilderness, it shifts to, "Lord, guide me into what's next. Show me how to steward what You've done in me."

   Pray like this:
   > "What in me has changed, Lord?"
   > "What assignments are waiting for this new version of me?"
   > "Where do I need to walk in faith before I see the fruit?"
   > *"What doors are You opening?"*

> *"What habits do You want me to carry forward?"*
> *"Who am I called to impact in this new season?"*
> "Lord, help me walk boldly in what You've prepared me for."
> "Reveal the doors You've opened, and give me the discernment to walk through them."
> "Let me carry the fire of the hidden place into every room You send me to."

Prayer becomes your GPS, not just your lifeline. It becomes more about partnering with revelation than begging for rescue.

3) **Move at the Pace of Grace.** Just because you're out of the wilderness doesn't mean you should sprint. Move with intention. Don't try to "catch up" to others—**you're on divine timing.**

Ask: *What's my next faithful step?*

Obedience in motion will always be better than perfection in pause.

4) **Start Building—Don't Wait for Perfect Conditions.** God doesn't refine you just to restore you—He refines you to **release you.**

Now is the time to:
> Revisit dreams you shelved.
> Obey promptings you used to question.
> Take small, faithful steps toward the vision.

5) **Do Not Underestimate Small Beginnings.** Start where you are—with what you've got—and let God breathe on it.

6) **Surround Yourself with Purpose-Driven People.** Now that you're stepping into the light, your circle matters more than ever. Find people who speak into your purpose—not your past. Stay close to those who see your calling and hold you accountable to your growth.

7) **Recognize What's Changed in You.** You're not the same person who entered the wilderness. Take time to notice the transformation: After a wilderness season, you may notice:
   > A greater peace in uncertainty.
   > A new hunger for God's presence.
   > A deeper clarity about what matters.
   > Less attachment to performance, people-pleasing, or pride.
   > Journal through questions like:
   > *What am I no longer willing to tolerate?*
   > *What used to scare me that no longer does?*
   > *What burdens me now that didn't before?* These are clues to your next assignment.
   > Am I slower to react and quicker to pray?
   > Do I crave God's presence more than people's approval?
   > Have I lost the taste for distractions that once consumed me?

   These aren't small shifts—they're spiritual upgrades. Take inventory of the growth. Don't ignore the fruit of your refining. Let your new identity inform your new direction.

8) **Walk in Bold Obedience.** Your emergence isn't about "feeling confident"—it's about trusting the One who brought you through. God didn't pull you from the fire to hide you again. He's calling you to speak, build, serve, create, lead—whatever aligns with the refining you just walked through. Don't go back to hiding. Don't downplay your testimony. Your wilderness was never wasted.

9) **Guard Your Circle—Find Vision Carriers.** Now more than ever, your circle matters. You can't afford to surround yourself with people who only knew the *old you*. Seek out voices who:

> See who you've become
> Call out your purpose
> Keep you grounded in truth

You need **vision carriers**, not spectators. Find people who sharpen your spirit and hold you accountable to your growth. The wrong circle can pull you back into hiding—but the right one will push you toward your unveiling.

10) **Expect Opposition but Stay Anchored.** Elevation often invites resistance. Don't be surprised if old fears resurface or new challenges arise. This isn't a sign that you're off course—it's confirmation that your movement matters. What God refines, the enemy tries to resist—but he cannot reverse it. Stay anchored in what God spoke to you in the dark. Return to the promises He whispered when no one was watching. Let your foundation be rooted in truth, not applause. And when you stay anchored in God's truth, you begin to see something remarkable—what once felt unreachable starts to come within view.

It's in that steadfast anchoring—despite resistance—that breakthrough begins to take shape, transforming what once seemed impossible into the possible.

THE UNACHIEVABLE BECAME ACHIEVABLE

Throughout history, the road to success has been paved with rejection, failure, and setbacks. Many of the world's greatest visionaries faced insurmountable challenges that would have discouraged most people. Yet, what set them apart was their resilience, unwavering belief, and refusal to quit.

Like an eagle soaring against strong winds, these individuals refused to let defeat ground them. They embraced their failures as stepping stones rather than roadblocks. Their persistence turned what seemed impossible into reality.

Mark Victor Hansen and Jack Canfield: The Chicken Soup for the Soul Series[26]

Before their book series became a global phenomenon, Mark Victor Hansen and Jack Canfield faced 140 rejections from publishers. Even their literary agent doubted them, returning their manuscript because he believed it was unsellable. But they refused to accept failure as the final answer. Today, their Chicken Soup for the Soul series has sold over 100 million copies worldwide.

The Wright Brothers: The Dream of Flight

Before the Wright brothers invented modern aviation and changed history, they experienced thousands of failed experiments. Their early attempts at flying were described as disappointing and uncontrollable. Many experts dismissed their vision as an impossible dream. But they persisted, making history and proving that man could soar—just as eagles do.

Stephen R. Covey: The Price of Leadership

Stephen R. Covey, author of *The 7 Habits of Highly Effective People*,[27] built one of the most influential leadership companies in the world. But before his company became a $160 million enterprise, it endured eleven straight years of financial struggle. With

---

26 Mark Victor Hansen and Jack Canfield, *Chicken Soup for the Soul (Series)* (1993-2007).
27 Stephen R. Covey, *The 7 Habits of Highly Effective People* (New York, NY: Free Press, 2004).

no money in the bank, maxed-out credit lines, and overwhelming debt, quitting would have been an easy choice. But Covey pressed on, proving that perseverance turns vision into victory.

Sam Walton: The Birth of Walmart

Before founding Walmart, Sam Walton lost his first store after five years of hard work. He described that moment as the lowest point of his business life, a devastating experience that left him feeling sick to his stomach. Yet rather than letting failure define him, he chose to rise again—this time with greater wisdom. Today, Walmart is one of the most successful retailers in the world, all because Walton refused to let one failure determine his future.

Colonel Sanders: The Recipe for Success

Before Kentucky Fried Chicken (KFC) became a household name, Colonel Sanders was rejected 1,009 times while trying to sell his fried chicken recipe. He was told "no" over one thousand times, yet he didn't stop knocking on doors. Finally, one restaurant gave him a chance, and the rest is history. By age seventy-four, he had over six hundred franchises, and today, KFC operates in over eighty countries, serving millions daily.

Sylvester Stallone: Fighting for His Dream

Before Sylvester Stallone became a Hollywood legend, he failed to sell his first eight screenplays, and over six hundred casting agents rejected him. Inspired by a boxing match between Muhammad Ali and Chuck Wepner, Stallone wrote the script for *Rocky*. Though rejected multiple times, he eventually sold the script, and *Rocky* went on to earn $117 million at the box office—turning Stallone into a star.

THE COMMON DENOMINATOR

Every single one of these individuals had valid reasons to give up—but they didn't. Instead, they embraced their struggles, learned from their failures, and persisted until the unachievable became achievable.

FINAL THOUGHT: DON'T JUST EMERGE—ENGAGE

Coming out of the wilderness isn't just about *being seen*—it's about being **sent**. You didn't endure the hidden place just to resume life as usual.

God didn't refine you for comfort—He refined you for calling.

So, don't waste the wilderness. Don't silence the lessons. Don't dismiss the strength you gained. Let what was formed in the fire **fuel your future**.

This is your moment not just to come out but to **step forward**—not just to be known but to **be useful**. Not just to survive but to **lead**.

Not just to be free but to **set others free**.

You're not just walking out of something. **You're walking into everything God has been preparing for you.**

From hidden to heralded—

Now, *walk like it.*

> Your time has come. Let's step into it.
> Unshakable faith isn't the absence of storms—
> it's the secret architecture that turns
> every howling wind into
> an elevator to new heights.
> —Tessy Tanyi

In the final chapter, we will explore what it means to step boldly into your divine identity and walk in the fullness of your calling. This is not just about surviving life's challenges or even thriving despite them—it's about reigning. It's about living a life of purpose, authority, and power, fully aligned with God's kingdom.

So, as you turn the page, prepare to spread your wings and take your rightful place in the skies. The journey ahead isn't just about soaring—it's about ruling with confidence, boldness, and divine purpose.

CHAPTER 17

THE MAJESTIC EAGLE

Welcome to Your Kingdom Living

Taking flight is only the beginning. Once you've embraced your identity, prepared your heart, and stepped into your calling, God invites you to thrive. Thriving as a kingdom eagle means soaring into a life of continual growth, impact, and purpose. It's about navigating the winds of change, facing challenges with confidence, and lifting others along the way. At this stage of your journey, you are no longer just discovering who you are—you are living it out. You have gone through the wilderness, endured the tests, and gained wisdom along the way. Now, it is time to soar boldly, embracing the fullness of your calling. This chapter provides six strategies that you can apply to enjoy God's fullest as you soar.

1) Rest in God's Presence: The Secret of Sustainable Soaring

Eagles don't fatigue themselves with frantic flapping—they ride the currents.

They find refuge in high places, safe from predators and the chaos below. In the same way, your spiritual endurance depends on anchoring yourself in God's presence. Thriving as a kingdom eagle means knowing when to rest in God's presence, allowing Him to renew your strength. Jesus reminds us of this in Matthew 11:28-30: "Come to me, all you who are weary and burdened, and I will give you rest. Take my yoke upon you and learn from me, for I am gentle and humble in heart, and you will find rest for your souls."

There was a season in my life when I felt completely drained. I was doing all the right things—serving, working, even spending time with God—but I wasn't allowing myself to truly rest in His presence. One day, during a quiet time, I sensed Him whisper, "Stop striving. Just be with Me." It was a simple yet profound moment. I sat in silence, letting His peace wash over me, and for the first time in a long while, I felt truly refreshed.

> *Eagles may fly high, but they nest together.*

Thus, as you soar:
- » Set aside time each day to rest in God's presence—whether through quiet prayer, worship, or simply sitting in silence.
- » Reflect on Matthew 11:28-30 and ask God to show you areas where you need to let go of burdens and find true rest in Him.

2) Soar in Covenant Community: The Strength of the Flock
Eagles may fly high, but they nest together.

Isolation is the enemy of elevation. While eagles are often known for flying alone, they thrive in their environment. Similarly, as believers, we are called to soar in the context of community—not in isolation. God uses relationships to encourage, challenge, and strengthen us. Hebrews 10:24-25 reminds us: "And let us consider how we may spur one another on toward love and good deeds, not giving up meeting together, as some are in the habit of doing, but encouraging one another—and all the more as you see the Day approaching."

For a long time, I believed I could handle life on my own. I kept my struggles to myself, afraid to appear weak. But as I opened up to trusted friends and mentors, I experienced the power of community. I learned to plan time for intentional fellowship and cultivate relationships that sharpen my vision (Hebrews 10:24-25). I also learned to practice vulnerability—letting trusted companions see my struggles—and their prayers became my updraft. They spoke truth into my life, prayed for me, and reminded me of God's promises when I couldn't see them myself. As you soar:

» Identify people in your life who can be part of your spiritual community. Reach out and invest in those relationships.

» If you don't have a strong community, pray for God to lead you to one. Consider joining a small group, a mentorship program, or a fellowship of believers.

3) Multiply Your Legacy: Training the Next Generation of Eagles
True eagles reproduce their strength—your breakthroughs are blueprints for others.

Mentor relentlessly: invest in at least one person who needs your wisdom (2 Timothy 2:2). Embrace storytelling. Share your wilderness testimonies—they're someone else's survival guide.

Thriving as a kingdom eagle means helping others discover their identity and purpose. Your journey is not just for you—it is meant to inspire and uplift those around you. God's heart cry is for kingdom eagles to rise up!! Second Timothy 2:2 says: "And the things you have heard me say in the presence of many witnesses entrust to reliable people who will also be qualified to teach others." This highlights the importance of sharing what you have learned—mentoring, teaching, and encouraging others to take flight in their own spiritual journeys.

I'll never forget the first time someone told me that my story impacted their life. It was a story of victory but came with struggle and God's faithfulness. Knowing that my difficult moments had a purpose beyond myself was life-changing. It reminded me that even in our hardest seasons, God is writing a greater story. Will you let God be glorified in your story?

» **Reflect on your own journey.** How has God worked in your life? Who might benefit from hearing your story?
» **Pray for opportunities to encourage and mentor others.** Be open to the Holy Spirit's leading in conversations and relationships.

4) Live the Eagle Life Daily: The Discipline of Dominion

Abundance isn't a destination—it's a daily posture.

Thriving isn't about reaching a final destination—it's about making each day count. The eagle life is a daily choice to soar, rest, and grow in God. John 10:10 reminds us: "I have come that they may have life, and have it to the full." This abundant life is not about material success but about living in the fullness of God's love, joy, and purpose.

From my own experience, some days, thriving feels easy. Other days, it feels like a struggle. But I've learned that thriving is not about how I feel—it's about choosing to trust God's plan, even on the hard days. It's about finding joy in the small things, staying connected to Him, and keeping my eyes on the bigger picture.

What I do to help me soar daily is this:

» Start each day by declaring God's promises over my life.
» Remind myself of His love, purpose, and strength.
» Look for ways to bring joy and purpose into my routine—through acts of kindness, moments of gratitude, and being present with God.

5) Break Barriers—Live Beyond Limits

Your barriers are training tools—not permanent boundaries.

We all have self-imposed limits—whether they come from fear, past failures, or the opinions of others. But God calls us to live beyond those limits and step into the fullness of His plan. Philippians 4:13 (NKJV) reminds us: "I can do all things through Christ who strengthens me." This is not just a motivational phrase—it is a promise. As shared in one of the preceding chapters of this book, one of my biggest personal barriers was fear of failure. I hesitated to take risks because I was afraid of making mistakes or letting people down. But God showed me that failure is not the enemy—fear is. As I step out in faith each day, I experience His strength in ways I never could have imagined.

Thus, I would like you to:
- » Identify one area where you feel limited. Bring it to God in prayer and ask Him for boldness.
- » Take a small step of faith this week, trusting God to lead and strengthen you.

6) Walk in Authority and Purpose

You carry heaven's mandate—not to beg for miracles but to command them.

Eagles do not hesitate—they soar with authority. As a follower of Christ, you have been given authority and purpose. Matthew 28:18-20 says: "All authority in heaven and on earth has been given to me. Therefore go and make disciples of all nations. . . . And surely I am with you always, to the very end of the age." There was a pivotal moment in my life when I realized I had been walking in disobedience because I was waiting for all the resources to come together before I embarked on what God was asking me to do. But God reminded me that His call was enough, and all I needed was to say yes and obey His voice. When I said yes to Him and stepped out in faith, I saw doors open and lives impacted in ways I never imagined. At this moment, I would like for you to pause:

- » Reflect on areas where God is calling you to step out in boldness.
- » Ask yourself the question: what's holding me back? Identify and write it down.
- » Write a declaration of truth about your authority and purpose. Speak it over yourself daily, and make up your mind to believe the truth more than the lies.
- » Step out and experience the SUPERNATURAL!!!

This is your final boarding call, royalty.
The ground has been your classroom,
but the sky is your kingdom.
Stop visiting your destiny.
Start inhabiting it.
—Tessy Tanyi

CHAPTER 18

FINAL CHARGE

Take Flight and Soar Above the Noise

As this journey comes to a close, take a moment to reflect on how far you've come. You have broken free from the limitations of a "chicken mentality" and embraced your true identity as an eagle Christian. You have endured the wilderness, strengthened your resilience, and built an unshakable faith. You have learned to guard your heart, feed on God's truth, and rise above the noise of the world.

This book has been more than just a roadmap—it has been an invitation. An invitation to unshackle your wings, step fully into your divine identity, and soar beyond every obstacle, distraction, and limitation that once held you back. You are no longer bound by your past, your struggles, or the opinions of others. You are an eagle created to dominate the skies and live a life of purpose, power, and freedom.

But this is not the end—it is only the beginning. The wisdom you have gained, the faith you have cultivated, and the truths you have embraced form the foundation for the extraordinary life God has prepared for you. A life of kingdom living, where you reign with authority, move in confidence, and fulfill your divine calling.

So, as you turn the final pages, hold onto this truth: **the skies are yours to claim.** The noise of the world may still be loud, but it no longer controls you. You now have the vision, the strength, and the faith to rise above it all.

Spread your wings, dear reader. The world is waiting for the majestic eagle you were always meant to be.

Welcome to your kingdom living.

The journey of an eagle Christian is not just about knowing who you are—it is about living boldly in that identity. It is not enough to admire the eagles, to be inspired by their strength, vision, and ability to rise above the storm. You were made to be one.

> *When you surrender your "security blanket" to God, He replaces it with a security that can't be hacked.*

The time for hesitation is over.
The time for playing small is over.
The time for blending in is over.
It's time to soar.

I'll never forget the day I left my IT career to follow God's call. For years, I sat trapped between two worlds—by day, I served as an IT Project Manager, overseeing systems and firewall operations. By night, I stepped into my calling as a preacher, serving, preparing sermons, or witnessing God shatter chains and transform broken lives. Every paycheck from my IT job felt like both a blessing and a betrayal of my true calling. I'll never forget the night Jennifer broke down. She'd been a familiar face at church for years—faithfully serving on the hospitality team, always in her seat on Sundays. But as I preached about the difference between religion and relationship, her carefully maintained facade crumbled. This poised young woman who'd mastered the routines of church suddenly collapsed at the altar, her tears washing away years of performance.

"I've been doing all the right things," she sobbed, her voice raw with revelation, "but tonight's the first time I actually want to know God—not just serve in His house." Her shaking hands clutched at her addiction recovery chips as she whispered, "I need Him to be real for me."

As I listened to her words, the Holy Spirit spoke with unmistakable clarity: *You're managing computer systems when I've called you to transform human souls.* Months later, I walked out of my corporate office for the last time.

The fear was paralyzing. My husband and I had a mortgage, bills piling up, and responsibilities that couldn't be ignored.

"Be practical," well-meaning friends cautioned. "Ministry won't pay your electricity bill." Some called it reckless. Others questioned my judgment and cautioned me to play it safe. But when I thought of Jennifer, six months later—sober, baptized, and leading others to freedom—I understood: when you surrender your "security blanket" to God, He replaces it with a security that can't be hacked. Ever since then, God has never let a bill go unpaid and has never failed to provide, and every time I see the gospel transform someone's life, I hear His gentle reminder: *This is why I called you out of the walled conference rooms and into My harvest field.*

FORGIVING THOSE WHO MISJUDGED MY CALLING

Another story I'll never forget is the suffocating heat of an August afternoon when a spiritual leader—a woman I'd served under for years—leaned across her desk and spoke words that nearly broke me: "Without me, you'll never fulfill your destiny. What you call 'ministry' is just spiritualized laziness."

The air left my lungs. This wasn't just criticism—it was a curse over my calling. For weeks, I paced my prayer closet rehearsing scathing rebuttals, compiling lists of her shortcomings to throw back in her face. Then, one morning during worship, God interrupted my rage with a vision: an eagle—majestic wings spread—desperately flapping but going nowhere. A rusted barnyard chain snared its talon, the other end buried in the dirt where chickens pecked. The revelation hit me like lightning: *You're letting her words tether you to the barnyard. Cut the chain.* Trembling, I scheduled a meeting with her and said what the Holy Spirit dictated.

Instead of defending myself, I said, "Thank you for what you've poured into me. Thank you for your rejection as it has forced me to find my worth in Christ alone. But as of today, I release myself from your spiritual control. I answer to heaven first." Her stunned silence spoke volumes.

That afternoon, I journaled: *People will misunderstand your anointing because they've only seen you in the barnyard. Fly anyway.* The freedom that followed was supernatural—when I stopped demanding earthly validation, I discovered heavenly acceleration. Within months, doors opened no man could've orchestrated.

When I left the meeting room, something supernatural happened—not in her but in me. An invisible weight lifted off my shoulders. The next time I shared the gospel, I preached with an authority I'd never known. Weeks later, that same pastor attended my service and publicly apologized.

Now, when I mentor young ministers, I tell them, "Some voices aren't covering—they're cages. Eagles don't need chickens to validate their wings. So, choose your mentors wisely."

I've learned that when we silence the limiting voices, we start to hear the ones that matter—voices of courage, faith, and resilience. That's why I want to share stories like Amanda's—stories that remind us what happens when people choose to soar, even when the odds say they shouldn't.

HOW AMANDA SOARED ABOVE CANCER

A friend of mine named Sarah shared with me the story of her dear, close friend, Amanda. Amanda's Stage IV diagnosis came on a Tuesday. By Friday, doctors said she had only six months to live. However, during a visit to her hospital room one day, Sarah found her scribbling in a journal titled "My Eagle Lessons."

Amanda told Sarah, "Psalm 103:5 says that God renews our youth like eagles." Sarah leaned in and asked, "So, what do eagles know that we don't?" The question stayed with Amanda. As she reflected, she discovered that eagles use storms to reach higher altitudes. That day, she started making a list:

1) **Chemo winds** = Spiritual altitude adjustment
2) **Weakness** = Training for God-reliance
3) **Pain** = Reminder this isn't home

Amanda lived three-and-a-half more years—long enough to see her son graduate and launch a patient ministry that's led more than 1,200 people to Christ. At her memorial service, one hundred white balloons were released. As they soared, her final journal entry was read aloud: *"Don't waste your storms. Soar."*

FROM TERMINAL TO TRIUMPH: GREGORY'S UNLIKELY HEALING

Gregory (name changed for privacy), a thirty-eight-year-old construction worker and father of three, never expected what started as a minor backache to turn his life upside down. Doctors delivered a crushing blow in 2021: Stage IV pancreatic cancer, with tumors spreading to his liver. The prognosis? Six to twelve months, even with aggressive treatment.

As chemotherapy ravaged his body, Gregory's spirit wavered. One night, too weak to stand, he lay in bed scrolling through his phone when a sermon clip caught his attention: "God doesn't need perfect faith—just surrendered trust."

> *You were never meant to cower in the shadow of death—you were born to soar on the winds of faith.*

That moment, he whispered, *Jesus, if You're real, show me. I'll still love You—whatever You give, whether healing or heaven—however, I want your healing.* A warmth flooded his chest, unlike anything he'd ever felt.

Three weeks later, Gregory's oncologist stared at the scans in disbelief:

- » Primary tumor shrunk by 70 percent
- » Liver metastases no longer active
- » Blood markers normalized

"Medically, this shouldn't happen," his doctor admitted. By his next checkup, Gregory was declared cancer-free—a result his medical team could only call "remarkable." Today, he leads a men's group at his church, mentoring others facing impossible battles.

> *"My healing wasn't because I had great faith but because God has great power. Whether He heals you here or in eternity—He's still good."*
>
> —Gregory

Gregory's story proves what this entire book has declared: you were never meant to cower in the shadow of death—you were born to soar on the winds of faith. Now, dear eagle, the sky awaits your wings.

As you've walked through the pages of this book, you have been given divine insight, wisdom, and revelation about what it truly means to live as an eagle Christian. You've learned about breaking free from the chicken mentality, overcoming the wilderness, developing resilience, and walking in kingdom authority. But now comes the most important question:

God isn't waiting for you to feel ready—He's waiting for you to respond.

What will you do with what you have learned?

Will this book remain just words on a page, or will it become the catalyst for transformation in your life? Too many believers read about faith but never act on it. Too many people dream about the life God has for them but never take the steps to live it. If you do not apply what you have learned, you will remain in the same place—stuck in the barnyard while God is calling you to the skies.

Knowledge without action is wasted potential. But those who take the truth they've received and put it into action will experience supernatural acceleration, divine favor, and unlimited possibilities in Christ.

THE COST OF STAYING GROUNDED

Staying where you are *feels* safe—but it steals what God designed for you. An eagle that refuses to fly doesn't just miss the view; it starves its purpose. Likewise, if fear or complacency keeps you grounded:

» Potential withers (you were made for more).
» Impact fades (the world needs your voice, not your silence).
» Faith stagnates (you'll never witness miracles from the nest).

This isn't a warning—it's an invitation.

God isn't waiting for you to feel ready—He's waiting for you to respond. You've heard the call. You've felt the stirring. Now it's time to act. Boldness isn't a personality trait—it's a decision. And now is the moment to decide.

Don't just read this—live it.

> *Hell doesn't tremble at your good intentions. It trembles at your obedience.*

Inspiration fades by tomorrow if you don't act today. You don't need perfect conditions—just the courage to spread your wings now. God isn't waiting for your fear to disappear; He's waiting for you to trust Him in spite of it (Isaiah 41:10).

Break free. Rise up. Then, turn and help someone else fly.

The enemy doesn't fear your highlights—he fears your obedience. What will you do before the day ends?

Below are five proven keys to rise above fear and soar. Don't overthink it—pick one and start within the next twenty-four hours.

1) **Name What's Holding You Down**
   > Write *one* fear or lie you've believed (e.g., "I'm not ready," "People will judge me").
   > Counter it with God's truth (e.g., "God equips the called"—Exodus 4:12).

2) **Fuel Your Flight**
   > **Prayer:** Start with five minutes a day—ask, "God, what's one thing You want me to do this week?"
   > **Word:** Read Ephesians 3:14–21. Circle every promise about God's power in you.

3) **Take a Twenty-Four-Hour Step of Faith**
   > Say "yes" to something that scares you *but aligns with God's Word* (e.g., confess a dream to a mentor; serve in a new way).

4) **Build an Eagle Squad**
   > Text *one* person who challenges you spiritually: "I'm stepping out in faith this week. Keep me accountable?"

5) **Help Someone Else Fly**
   > Share *one* lesson from this chapter with someone struggling—today.

THE SKY IS YOUR STARTING LINE

God isn't waiting for you to be perfect. He's waiting for you to *move*.
"Now to Him who is able to do immeasurably more. . . ."
—Ephesians 3:20

Your next step isn't a question—it's an assignment. Write it down. Do it before sunset.

Now—before you close this book—do one thing above. Not tomorrow. Not "when you're ready." Today. Hell doesn't tremble at your good intentions. It trembles at your obedience.

Your time is now. Soar.

PROPHETIC DECLARATIONS

As you step into your eagle Christian identity, declare these truths:

- » I am not a chicken—I am an eagle. I was made to soar!
- » I refuse to live in fear, doubt, or limitations.
- » I walk in kingdom authority and divine purpose.
- » I am strong, courageous, and bold in the Lord.
- » I embrace my God-given destiny with confidence.
- » I am an overcomer. No weapon formed against me shall prosper.
- » I will rise above every storm and fulfill my purpose.
- » I will not die until I have truly lived the life God created me for.

Soar into your destiny!
You have been trained.
You have been equipped.
You have been prepared.
Now, the world is waiting for you.
So, lift your wings.
Take a deep breath.
And SOAR!
Your Time Is Now.
No more excuses.

No more delays.

No more holding back.

Let this be the moment you look back on and say, "This is when everything changed."

God is calling.

The wind is beneath you.

Now . . . SOAR!

The runway of preparation ends here.

The lies that clipped your wings lie in ashes.

The cage door swings wide on redeemed hinges.

Now hear your final boarding call, eagle:

> You were never meant to merely survive—
> you were forged to dominate skies.
> The world's noise will always scream for your attention,
> but your true altitude is found
> only in the sound of your Maker's voice.
> So, flap once more.
> Leap.
> And discover what your wings already know.
> —Your fellow sky-dweller

ABOUT THE AUTHOR

Tessy Tanyi is a fiery voice of awakening, calling readers to shed fear and own their identity as anointed, unstoppable kingdom leaders. With theological training and prophetic urgency, she equips believers to trade barnyard mentalities for kingdom impact. A writer, speaker, and spiritual midwife, she doesn't just inspire—**she ignites transformation**, wielding truth to dismantle complacency and fuel bold action. Through books, sermons, or conversations, her message rings clear: you carry divine power—rise and release it. Off-duty, she's adventuring with family or cheering on fellow eagles. The barnyard is behind you. **The sky is yours—soar.**

Connect: tessytanyi.org

www.ingramcontent.com/pod-product-compliance
Lightning Source LLC
Chambersburg PA
CBHW050855160426
43194CB00011B/2161